The Complete Beginner's Guide To ChatGPT

Master Practical AI and Effective Prompts to Gain an Edge in Just 7 Days

Contents

Get Your Free Guide: 10 Ways to Make Money with AI!

To thank you for reading this book and to help you get the most out of the tools and exercises you'll find here, I want to offer you something special. I've created a free guide that reveals 10 breakthrough strategies for making money with AI.

Not only will this guide provide you with ideas, but it will also complement the exercises in this book, giving you even more tools to apply what you learn right away. As you work through the activities and explore the opportunities that artificial intelligence can offer you, you can start thinking about how to implement these strategies in your own life or business.

Download your free guide now by clicking or scanning the QR code:

Introduction

I magine the sense of empowerment and accomplishment you could feel by mastering a powerful AI tool like ChatGPT in just a week. Let me share a quick story: Sarah, a small business owner, struggled to keep up with customer inquiries and manage her marketing efforts effectively. After dedicating one week to fully understanding and integrating ChatGPT into her business, she saw a remarkable transformation. She automated customer service, freeing up valuable time, and created personalized marketing content that significantly boosted her engagement rates. This achievement improved her business and instilled a sense of empowerment and accomplishment. You, too, can experience this by embarking on the same journey.

ChatGPT is a game-changing AI technology that is reshaping industries and can be mastered in just seven days. If you're new to AI, the idea might seem intimidating, but rest assured, it's more within your reach than you think. This guide is tailored to take you from a curious beginner to a confident user, dedicating a small portion of your day for one week to understanding and applying ChatGPT. You'll be pleasantly surprised at how practical and straightforward the learning journey can be.

My vision for this guide is simple: to break down the barriers of AI and make ChatGPT approachable and valuable for you. Whether you're looking to enhance your professional skills, streamline tasks, or satisfy your curiosity about

AI, this book promises to equip you with the necessary knowledge and skills to make a tangible difference in your life.

You, the reader, might be someone overwhelmed by technology, a busy professional looking for efficiency, or a lifelong learner eager to explore new tools. No matter your background, this book is crafted for your success. It's structured to provide a practical, engaging, and empowering journey through the world of AI, with each day's learning designed to build on the previous one.

Think of this book as a week-long conversation with a supportive friend who's there to guide you through the complexities of AI. The style of this book is conversational and optimistic, designed to keep things light, engaging, and, most importantly, understandable. There is no jargon, no overwhelming details—just clear, actionable steps that lead to actual results. You'll feel comfortable and at ease, as you embark on this journey with a supportive companion.

We'll start with the basics of AI and ChatGPT and quickly move into practical applications. By the end of the week, we'll explore some advanced features and ethical considerations. Each chapter includes hands-on exercises to reinforce what you've learned and see the technology in action.

On a personal note, my journey into AI started much like yours might today - curious and a bit unsure. Within a week of diving into ChatGPT, I was fascinated and saw significant improvements in managing my tasks and information. This experience ignited my passion to share these benefits with others, especially those who might feel hesitant about stepping into AI.

The 7-Day Structure: Mastery in One Week

The book is structured into seven chapters to make your journey effective and manageable. Each chapter represents one day of focused learning, designed to help you build upon the previous day's knowledge, leading you to master ChatGPT by the end of the week.

On **Day 1**, you will lay the groundwork by understanding the foundational concepts of AI and ChatGPT. This day is all about simplifying the technology and preparing you for the more detailed applications that will follow. By the end of this day, you'll have a solid grasp of ChatGPT and how it works, setting the stage for the rest of the week.

Day 2 focuses on mastering the skill of prompt engineering, which essentially means crafting clear and precise instructions to receive the best responses. This skill is crucial as it helps you frame the right questions to get the most accurate results. By the end of this day, you'll be able to create effective prompts that enhance your interaction with ChatGPT, ensuring you get the most useful output.

On **Day 3**, you'll explore how ChatGPT can enhance business productivity. From managing emails to optimizing customer service and creating content, you'll discover practical ways to integrate ChatGPT into your business work-flows, improving creativity, efficiency, and productivity. This day will show you how to leverage AI to streamline your professional tasks.

Day 4 shifts focus to your personal life. You'll learn how to integrate ChatGPT into your daily routines, such as managing schedules, enhancing health and wellness, and budgeting. By the end of this day, you'll see how ChatGPT can simplify and enrich your life, making everyday tasks more manageable.

On **Day 5**, the focus will shift to ethical use and the social implications of AI. You'll gain an understanding of the ethical considerations and societal impact of using technologies like ChatGPT. This day will guide you on using ChatGPT responsibly and thoughtfully, making you aware of the broader implications of AI.

Day 6 is dedicated to exploring ChatGPT's advanced features and customiza-tion options. You'll explore its more sophisticated functionalities and learn how to tailor It to meet specific needs. By the end of day 6, you can customize Chat-

GPT's features to suit specialized tasks, enhancing its value and effectiveness for your unique applications.

Finally, on **Day 7**, you'll learn how to stay ahead with ChatGPT by keeping up with the evolving landscape of AI and continuously improving your skills. You'll be introduced to resources for ongoing learning and adaptation. By the end of this day, you'll be prepared to stay updated with the latest advancements in AI, ensuring you remain competitive and knowledgeable in this fast-evolving field.

So, are you ready to transform your understanding and use of AI technology in just one week? Let's get started on this exciting journey together. By the end of this book, you'll not only grasp the fundamentals of ChatGPT but also uncover its potential to enhance your daily life and work. Let's turn curiosity into capability, starting now!

Foundations of ChatGPT and AI

In the bustling world of technology, where innovation leaps from one break-through to another, it might surprise you that the most profound impacts often stem from understanding the basics. Artificial Intelligence, or AI, is one such fundamental that has been seamlessly woven into our daily lives, often without us noticing, enhancing our experiences and interactions in multiple ways. For instance, AI can provide instant weather updates and personalized recommendations on your favorite streaming service. This chapter aims to peel back the layers of complexity surrounding Artificial Intelligence, presenting a clear, simplified explanation tailored to those new to this vast and intriguing field.

1.1 What is AI? A Simplified Explanation for Non-Techies

Definition and Evolution

Artificial Intelligence, in its simplest form, refers to the capability of a machine to imitate intelligent human behavior. Unlike traditional machines, AI systems can learn from experience, adapt to new inputs, and perform human-like tasks. The concept of AI isn't new; it dates back to the ancient myths of mechanical men designed to mimic our behavior. However, the journey of AI as we understand it today began in the mid-20th century, rooted in the question posed by a pioneer in computing, Alan Turing: "Can machines think?"

Over the decades, AI has evolved from basic algorithms capable of simple tasks to complex systems that can drive cars, beat world champions in strategic games like chess and Go, and accurately diagnose diseases. In recent years, this evolution has been propelled by leaps in computing power and data availability, allowing machines to process and learn from vast amounts of information faster and more efficiently than humans.

Types of AI

Understanding the different types of Artificial Intelligence helps simplify the confusion surrounding its capabilities and limitations. Primarily, AI can be classified into three types:

1. <u>Narrow AI</u>: These systems are designed to handle a single or limited task. An example is facial recognition software that unlocks your smartphone. While sophisticated, it operates under a limited set of constraints and doesn't possess understanding or consciousness.

2. <u>General AI</u>: Often considered the holy grail of AI, general AI would have a wide-reaching intellect and cognitive abilities comparable to a human's. Such systems could perform any intellectual task with the same accuracy level as a human. However, general AI remains a largely theoretical concept at this stage.

3. <u>Superintelligent AI</u>: This type of AI goes beyond human intelligence, possessing cognitive skills superior to humans in practically all areas, including creativity, general wisdom, and problem-solving. Superintelligence is also theoretical and poses interesting questions for futurists and ethicists alike.

AI in Daily Life

Look around, and you'll find AI integrated into many aspects of your life. Personal assistants like Siri and Alexa are powered by AI and are designed to interpret your voice commands and assist with tasks. Recommendation systems, such as those used by Netflix and Amazon, analyze your past behavior to suggest products or movies you might like. Even more critically, AI is used to operate autonomous vehicles, which can sense their environment and navigate without human input.

Impact on Society

The implications of AI on society are profound and multifaceted. Economically, AI can lead to significant efficiencies and cost savings, driving growth in every industry, from manufacturing and finance to retail and entertainment. Socially, AI applications in healthcare, such as predictive diagnostics and personalized medicine, can save lives and improve quality of life. However, there are challenges, including job displacements due to automation and concerns about privacy and surveillance. The societal impact of AI necessitates a balanced approach to technology governance and ethical considerations, ensuring AI benefits are maximized while minimizing potential harm.

Understanding AI in these comprehensive yet accessible terms provides a foundation for technical mastery and appreciating the profound way it intersects with human endeavors and ethics. This understanding is crucial as we navigate the current landscapes of innovation and disruption these intelligent systems bring.

1.2 Understanding ChatGPT: From Basics to First Conversation

ChatGPT, developed by OpenAI, is a specific application of AI designed to simulate human-like conversations through text. It stands out as a technology engineered to process data and interact in a way that mimics human conversational patterns. This capability makes it an exceptional tool for various practical applications, from customer service and personalized tutoring to scientific research and fraud detection. As a conversational AI, ChatGPT's fundamental purpose is to provide responses that are not only accurate but also contextually relevant, making interactions feel natural and engaging.

At its core, ChatGPT utilizes a complex computer model trained on a massive dataset of text and code to process user inputs and generate responses that simulate human conversation. When you ask ChatGPT a question, it doesn't search the web for answers but instead draws on patterns and information it has learned during its training phase. Imagine this process as similar to how a well-read person might draw on their extensive reading experience to answer questions on various topics. They don't know everything, nor do they pull up specific articles they've read. Instead, they synthesize their accumulated knowledge to provide answers that make sense based on the context of the conversation.

ChatGPT's capabilities are distinctively different from more narrowly focused AI applications such as those used for image recognition or structured data analysis. Unlike these specialized AIs, ChatGPT is versatile in its knowledge base and application, making it broadly applicable across many scenarios where nuanced conversation is beneficial. This versatility is rooted in its foundational technology - the **Generative Pre-trained Transformer**, or GPT, which allows it to generate human-like text based on the prompts it receives.

For those eager to start interacting with ChatGPT, the process is straightforward. Initially, setting up an account with OpenAI or any platform offering access to ChatGPT is required. You're ready to begin your first conversation once you've created an account and logged in. Start with simple questions or prompts to understand how ChatGPT responds. For instance, you might type "Write me a poem." or "Tell me a joke." As you interact more, try asking more complex questions or exploring topics of personal interest to see how ChatGPT handles a wide range of subjects.

During these initial interactions, it's fascinating to observe how ChatGPT attempts to provide contextually appropriate responses. However, it's also crucial to understand that while ChatGPT can generate impressively coherent and context-aware responses, its knowledge is fixed when it was last trained. It doesn't have real-time access to the internet or updates on current events unless integrated with other tools that provide such data. This limitation is essential to remember as you explore this conversational AI's capabilities.

Engaging with ChatGPT can be a delightful and enlightening experience, especially as you understand the depth and breadth of conversations possible with this AI. Whether you're looking to solve a problem, gather information, or have an engaging chat, ChatGPT offers a window into the future of human-AI interaction, where machines can understand and respond to us with a level of relevance and immediacy that was once the stuff of science fiction. As you continue to explore, remember that each interaction with ChatGPT provides answers and helps you better understand the intricate dance between human queries and AI responses. This dynamic is continually reshaping our interaction with technology.

1.3 Decoding Machine Learning and Its Role in ChatGPT

Machine learning is a core pillar supporting artificial intelligence's vast, dynamic world. It's a field that allows computers to absorb and adapt to new data without being explicitly programmed to do so—an ability that might sound like something out of science fiction but is increasingly becoming a standard aspect of modern technology. At its heart, machine learning involves the development of algorithms that can analyze data, learn from it, and make predictions or decisions based on that knowledge. Imagine teaching your computer to recognize patterns like a human brain does; that's essentially what machine learning achieves. It's like educating your computer to predict outcomes based on past experiences, a process that evolves continuously through further interactions and data exposure.

Specifically, in the context of ChatGPT, machine learning is not just a feature; it's the backbone. ChatGPT learns from an extensive collection of text data from various sources. This training involves feeding it large amounts of data and allowing it to know and understand the nuances of human language. Every time you interact with ChatGPT, it's applying what it learned during its training phase to generate contextually appropriate responses. For instance, when you ask ChatGPT about the weather, it doesn't look up real-time online weather reports; instead, it generates a response based on patterns and information it has learned from its training data, which does not include current weather information. This ability to generate human-like text based on learned data without direct access to or reliance on real-time data distinguishes ChatGPT in AI applications.

Diving deeper into the types of machine learning models, three main categories are particularly relevant to AI development: supervised learning, unsupervised learning, and reinforcement learning. Supervised learning involves training a model on a labeled dataset, meaning each training example is paired with an output label. For instance, in teaching a model to differentiate between spam emails and those that are not, each email in the training set is tagged as 'spam' or 'not spam.' ChatGPT, however, primarily uses another sophisticated type of machine learning known as unsupervised learning, where the system learns to identify patterns and relationships in input data that isn't explicitly labeled.

Another intriguing area is reinforcement learning, which involves training models to make sequences of decisions by rewarding them for positive outcomes. This technique is not primarily used in ChatGPT but is crucial in other AI scenarios like gaming or navigation, where the AI must make decisions that build on one another toward a goal. Each of these learning types contributes uniquely to the abilities of AI systems, enabling them to handle tasks ranging from simple classification, such as identifying spam emails, to complex decision-making processes that mimic human thought, like planning an optimal delivery route for multiple packages in a dynamic environment.

To illustrate the impact of machine learning on ChatGPT's performance, consider how it adapts to new information over time. Early versions of such models might have struggled with specific linguistic nuances or cultural references. However, as they are exposed to more diverse data sets and feedback, their ability to understand and respond appropriately to a broader range of queries improves significantly. This ongoing learning process is vital for maintaining the relevance and usefulness of AI in a world where human conversations and cultural contexts are constantly evolving.

What sets machine learning apart from traditional rule-based systems in the practical application of technologies like ChatGPT is its ability to respond to queries and learn from the inputs it receives, refining its algorithms and enhancing its interactions with users. This capability ensures that AI technologies remain valuable and practical tools in our digital arsenal, supporting various activities, from everyday tasks like scheduling and information retrieval to more complex operations such as automated customer service and content creation. As we continue to integrate AI into various facets of life and work, understanding machine learning will be crucial for anyone looking to optimize these interactions and harness the full potential of this transformative technology.

1.4 The Essentials of Natural Language Processing (NLP)

Natural Language Processing, or NLP, is a fascinating facet of artificial intelligence that focuses on the interaction between computers and humans through language. It's essentially about enhancing how technology understands and responds to human language in a natural and effective way. NLP is not just about programming computers to comprehend words and sentences; it's about enabling them to grasp the nuances and contexts of language as we do, which is a pivotal step towards making human-computer interactions as smooth and natural as possible.

At its core, NLP involves various techniques to bridge the gap between human communication and machine understanding. One of the foundational techniques is tokenization. This process consists of breaking down text into smaller parts, such as words or phrases, making it easier for the machine to understand and process. For example, the sentence "ChatGPT is helpful" would be split into tokens: 'ChatGPT,' 'is,' and 'helpful.' This breakdown process is similar to how we naturally pause and emphasize certain words in our speech to convey meaning more clearly. By tokenizing text, computers can start to analyze and interpret language in a structured, logical way, which is crucial for all subsequent NLP tasks.

Another significant NLP technique is sentiment analysis. This involves determining the emotional tone behind a series of words used to gain an understanding of the attitudes, opinions, and emotions expressed within an online comment. For instance, from the statement "I love ice cream," sentiment analysis tools can identify the positive sentiment associated with the message. Conversely, the statement "I hate traffic" would be recognized as conveying a negative sentiment. This ability to assess sentiments can be beneficial, particularly in fields like marketing and customer service, where understanding consumer emotions plays a crucial role in addressing their needs and concerns.

Named Entity Recognition (NER) is another crucial NLP technique that identifies and classifies critical text elements into predefined categories. For example, in the sentence "Einstein was born in Ulm," 'Einstein' would be recognized as a person and 'Ulm' as a location. This allows the computer to understand essential details in the text, enabling it to manage information more effectively. Whether extracting names from a large dataset or identifying locations mentioned in a tweet, NER helps structure and categorize text to enhance data retrieval and analysis processes.

These NLP techniques play a pivotal role in ChatGPT's functioning. By employing methods like tokenization, sentiment analysis, and named entity recognition, ChatGPT can understand a user's input, grasp the context and emotion of the conversation, and respond in a relevant and appropriate way. This ability makes ChatGPT an effective communication tool. It enhances its applications across various domains where understanding user sentiment is crucial or where recognizing key entities and themes can guide more targeted and effective outputs.

However, despite the advances in NLP, there are still challenges. One significant issue is dealing with ambiguity in language. Words with multiple meanings can confuse AI models if the context isn't unclear. For instance, the word "bat" can refer to a piece of sports equipment or an animal, and understanding which meaning is correct in a given sentence requires a sophisticated grasp of context. Another challenge is maintaining the context over more extended conversations, which is crucial for ensuring that the responses remain relevant and do not lose track of what has been discussed previously. For example, if someone mentions "Paris" early in a conversation and later refers to "the city," the system needs to remember that "the city" refers to "Paris."

These challenges underscore the complexity and sophistication required in NLP to mimic human-like understanding and response patterns. As technology evolves, the solutions to these challenges will refine how effectively computers can interact with human language, making our interactions with AI more seamless and intuitive. As we continue integrating AI into our daily lives, understanding and improving these NLP techniques will ensure that our interactions with technology are as rewarding and effective as possible.

1.5 Exploring Generative Pre-trained Transformers (GPT)

Understanding the intricacies of Generative Pre-trained Transformers, commonly known as GPT, is like peeling back the curtain on a Broadway stage to reveal the mechanisms that make the magic happen. Developed by OpenAI, GPT is an AI technology that excels in understanding and generating human-like text, paving the way for systems like ChatGPT. At its core, GPT is built on transformer architecture. This breakthrough has significantly advanced the field of machine learning by enhancing the model's ability to handle data sequences, such as sentences in a text.

The foundation of GPT lies in its ability to process and generate text based on patterns it has learned during its training. This is not just about recognizing words but understanding the context and the small, delicate, or intricate details of language that make communication meaningful. The architecture of GPT includes what are known as attention mechanisms. These mechanisms allow the model to weigh the importance of different words in a sentence, regardless of their position. For example, in the sentence "The cat that sat on the mat," the word 'cat' is crucial for understanding the subject, while 'on' links elements of the location. GPT's attention mechanism evaluates these relationships, enabling it to comprehend and generate coherent and contextually appropriate text.

Diving deeper into the architecture, GPT is structured in layers, and each process of the input text increases in complexity. Initially, the input text is split into tokens—similar to breaking a sentence into words and phrases—then embedded with numerical values representing different aspects of the language. These embeddings move through the network's layers, transforming them step-by-step, each layer building on the previous one's output. The final layer then generates text based on the transformed embeddings, which reflect a deep understanding of the input text's linguistic structure, style, and implied meanings.

The training process of GPT models is a two-stage journey involving pre-training and fine-tuning. During pre-training, the model is exposed to a vast amount of text data, learning the language's general patterns, grammar, and vocabulary. This stage is not specific to any particular task but aims to develop a broad understanding of the language. Following this, the fine-tuning stage adjusts the model to perform tasks like answering questions, translating languages, or writing content. Here, the model is trained on a smaller, task-specific dataset, allowing it to hone its skills and improve performance in particular applications.

Speaking of applications, the versatility of GPT extends far beyond generating conversational text for ChatGPT. Its ability to understand and produce text has been applied in various fields. In translation, GPT models can assist in converting text from one language to another, understanding the nuances and context often lost with more basic translation software. These models generate creative and informative articles in content creation, frequently starting from just a headline or a keyword prompt. Furthermore, GPT can summarize extensive documents efficiently, distilling long reports into concise summaries, which proves invaluable in fields like law and academia, where large volumes of text are expected.

These applications underscore the transformative potential of GPT across different sectors. By automating complex language tasks, GPT enhances productivity and opens new possibilities for human creativity and interaction. Whether it's helping a student understand a complex text, assisting a journalist in drafting articles, or enabling a lawyer to summarize cases quickly, GPT is reshaping how we interact with text and, by extension, with each other. As we continue to explore and develop this technology, its capacity to understand and interact with human language will increasingly blur the lines between human and machine-generated text, making our interactions with AI more natural and, ultimately, more human.

1.6 Ethical AI: Principles for Responsible Use

Having explored the foundations of AI and the intricacies of ChatGPT, it's crucial now to consider the ethical frameworks that ensure these technologies are used responsibly. Ethical AI involves creating systems that not only comply with legal standards but also operate within the moral expectations of society, ensuring they contribute positively and do not harm users or perpetuate unfair biases. This focus is essential because, as AI technologies become more integrated into our daily lives, their decisions can significantly impact individuals and communities. Ethical considerations are not just add-ons but foundational elements that guide AI technology's responsible development and use.

The principles of ethical AI include transparency, fairness, privacy, and accountability. Transparency in AI means that the operations and decisions of AI systems should be understandable by humans. This is particularly important in applications like ChatGPT, where users should be able to comprehend how the AI came up with its responses. Fairness involves ensuring that AI systems do not embed or perpetuate discrimination and are equitable in their operations. This can be challenging, as AI systems often learn from large datasets that may contain biased human decisions. Privacy is another cornerstone, requiring personal data used to train or operate AI systems to be handled securely and confidentially to protect user information. Lastly, accountability in AI systems means that there should be mechanisms in place to hold the developers and operators of AI systems responsible for how their systems operate.

ChatGPT, like many AI models, faces specific ethical challenges. One of the most significant issues is biases in training data. Because ChatGPT learns from a vast range of internet text, it can inadvertently learn and perpetuate the biases present in that data. This might manifest in gender, racial, or ideological biases that skew the AI's responses in ways that could be harmful or unfair. Another challenge is the potential misuse of conversational AIs. For instance, because ChatGPT can generate plausible human-like text, its application is risky in creating misleading or harmful content, such as fake news or impersonations.

Several best practices should be followed to mitigate these risks and ensure the ethical use of ChatGPT and similar AI systems. First, developers and users of AI systems should be trained in ethical AI practices. This includes education on the potential biases in AI systems and how to avoid or mitigate them. Second, regular audits of AI systems, particularly those like ChatGPT that learn from user interactions, are crucial. These audits can help identify and correct biases or other ethical issues that arise as the AI learns and evolves. Transparency is also vital; users should be informed about how the AI works and any limitations in its knowledge or capabilities. Finally, there should be clear guidelines and policies to prevent the misuse of AI technologies, coupled with robust security measures to protect data and prevent unauthorized access.

By adhering to these core ethical principles and best practices, developers and users of AI can help ensure that technologies like ChatGPT are used responsibly and beneficially. Ethical AI is about preventing harm and ensuring that AI technologies are aligned with society's broader values and needs, contributing positively to human progress and well-being. As we continue to develop and integrate AI into various aspects of life, maintaining a solid ethical framework will be essential to harness the benefits of AI while managing its challenges effectively.

1.7 Interactive Task: Set Up Your First ChatGPT Interaction

Embarking on your first interaction with ChatGPT is an exciting step into conversational AI. Let's begin by setting up your account. The process is straightforward and designed to be user-friendly, ensuring accessibility even for those who may not be tech-savvy. First, visit the OpenAI website or the platform where ChatGPT is hosted. Here, you will find an option to sign up or register. Typically, this involves entering basic information such as your name, email address, and password. Some platforms allow you to register by linking another social account, such as Google or Apple. Once your account is set up, you can log in and explore ChatGPT's capabilities.

Navigating the ChatGPT interface is the next step. Upon your first login, you'll likely be greeted by a clean, minimalistic interface with a prominent area to type your questions or prompts. This is the primary interaction space where your conversation with ChatGPT will unfold. Familiarize yourself with menus or settings options on the interface's edges. These may allow you to adjust preferences, manage your account, or access help resources. Taking a moment to click through these options can enhance your understanding and control of the interaction process.

Crafting your initial prompts is crucial in shaping the quality and relevance of ChatGPT's responses. A well-constructed prompt should be clear and direct, providing enough context to guide the AI in generating a precise and informative response. For example, instead of asking, "weather," which is vague and could result in a generic response, try "What is the current weather in Paris?" This prompt is specific and leads to a targeted response. Conversely, a poor prompt like "Paris weather now?" lacks clarity and might confuse the AI or lead to less accurate output. Remember, the clarity of your question significantly influences the effectiveness of ChatGPT's answers.

Interpreting responses from ChatGPT is another skill that enhances your interaction experience. Responses from ChatGPT can range from straightforward facts to more complex explanations, depending on your prompt. When evaluating responses, it's essential to recognize that ChatGPT, while sophisticated, has limitations. It generates responses based on patterns and data learned during training, which means it can occasionally produce incorrect or biased information, especially if the query involves subjective interpretation or is outside the scope of its training data. For instance, asking ChatGPT for advice on personal or medical issues might not yield reliable or safe information. It is crucial to critically assess the responses significantly when they influence decision-making or involve specialized knowledge areas.

As you interact more with ChatGPT, you'll notice patterns and learn how to phrase your questions to obtain the most accurate and relevant information. This practice will enhance your ability to use ChatGPT effectively and deepen your understanding of how AI interprets and processes human language. Remember, each interaction is an opportunity to refine your questioning skills and adapt based on the responses you receive. This iterative process is part of the fascinating journey of learning to communicate effectively with an AI, opening up new possibilities for information gathering, learning, and even entertainment. As you continue to explore and interact with ChatGPT, let your curiosity guide you toward discovering the vast capabilities and, occasionally, the quirky limitations of what AI can offer. Now that you have completed this interactive task reflect on your newfound skills and prepare for the exciting journey ahead as you dive deeper into mastering ChatGPT.

Mastering Prompt Engineering

Congratulations on completing Chapter One! Today, we take the next step in our seven-day journey by diving deeper into AI and exploring prompt engineering. Picture yourself in a master chef's kitchen, with the finest ingredients ready for you to create something extraordinary. Just like the quality of a dish depends on how you blend these ingredients, the success of ChatGPT interactions hinges on how you construct your prompts. This chapter is your guide to mastering prompt engineering, an essential skill enabling you to communicate effectively with ChatGPT. By honing this skill, you'll ensure that every exchange with ChatGPT is productive, insightful, and tailored to your needs.

2.1 Basics of Crafting Effective Prompts

Understanding Input Sensitivity

The specificity and structure of your prompts play a pivotal role in the quality of responses you receive from ChatGPT. This concept, called input sensitivity, is akin to tuning a musical instrument; the better the tuning, the sweeter the melody. When you provide ChatGPT with specific, well-structured prompts, you guide the AI to understand the topic at hand and the depth and angle of response you expect. For instance, a vague prompt like "Tell me about dogs" can lead to a generic response. In contrast, a specific prompt such as "What are the common health issues faced by Labrador Retrievers?" directs ChatGPT to generate a focused and detailed reply. The key lies in being precise with your questions, which helps the AI focus on its "thoughts" and deliver the necessary information.

Key Components of a Good Prompt

Creating an effective prompt involves several critical elements: clarity, focus, and context. Clarity means being explicit about what you want to know, leaving little room for misinterpretation. Focus is about narrowing down the subject to avoid overwhelming breadth, which can dilute the value of the response. Context ties your question to specific conditions or scenarios, enriching the AI's understanding and the relevance of its response. Together, these elements form a robust framework that enhances the interaction between you and ChatGPT, much like a well-written recipe guides a cook to culinary success.

Examples of Effective vs. Ineffective Prompts

To illustrate, consider these examples:

- **Ineffective:** "Book recommendation."

- **Effective:** "Recommend a thriller novel set in a dystopian future with strong female characters."

The first prompt is vague and lacks context, making it difficult for ChatGPT to provide a meaningful suggestion. However, The second prompt is clear and specific, allowing ChatGPT to provide a tailored and helpful recommendation.

- Ineffective: "Plan a holiday."

- Effective: "Could you suggest a 5-day itinerary for a family vacation in Paris, including kid-friendly activities?"

Here, the effective prompt provides a clear, focused, contextual framework, enabling ChatGPT to generate a targeted and practical response.

Initial Setup for Success

Before you even begin to type out your prompt, it's crucial to define the goal of your conversation with ChatGPT. What are you hoping to achieve? Are you looking for information, advice, or perhaps entertainment? Setting your goal will guide how you frame your prompt. Additionally, choosing the right tone and style for your prompt can significantly impact the interaction. For example, a formal tone might suit business-related queries, while a casual tone might be better for personal or less formal topics. This initial setup acts as your blueprint, ensuring that every element of your prompt contributes towards a meaningful and satisfying exchange with ChatGPT.

Crafting prompts might seem simple, but like any skill, it requires practice and attention to detail. As you spend more time interacting with ChatGPT, you'll develop a sharper sense of formulating your prompts to get the best out of this powerful tool. Each conversation is an opportunity to refine your technique and move closer to mastering the art of prompt engineering. This chapter sets the foundation for that mastery, providing the tools and understanding needed to create effective prompts that lead to rewarding interactions with AI. As you progress, remember that each prompt is a step towards deeper learning and greater confidence in your ability to leverage AI effectively in everyday life.

2.2 Advanced Prompt Techniques for Specific Outcomes

When you begin to feel more comfortable with the basics of crafting prompts for ChatGPT, you might find yourself curious about how to fine-tune your approach to achieve even more tailored and specific outcomes. This part of your learning curve involves using more sophisticated techniques that can significantly enhance the interaction quality and the utility of the responses you receive from ChatGPT. Let's explore some advanced techniques that can transform your prompts from simple questions into powerful tools that command detailed and contextually aware responses.

Conditional Prompting for Complex Requests

Conditional prompting is a technique where you structure your prompts to include specific conditions that must be met in the response. This method is particularly useful when dealing with complex requests where the output needs to reflect multiple variables or conditions. Consider it like setting several 'if' statements that guide ChatGPT's response process. For instance, if you are planning a trip and have several preferences – like budget, destination type, and activities – a conditional prompt might look like this, "Can you suggest a travel plan that stays under $3000, includes outdoor activities and is suitable for a family of four?" By specifying these conditions, you guide ChatGPT in tailoring its search and response strategy to meet all the criteria, making the information more relevant and useful.

Sequential Prompting for Detailed Explanations

Sequential prompting is about breaking down a complex request into a series of more straightforward prompts, which gradually build up to provide a detailed explanation or comprehensive response. This approach can be likened to teaching someone a new skill step-by-step. Each prompt is a building block, laying the foundation for more complex information. For example, suppose you want to understand how electric cars work. In that case, you might start with, "What is an electric car?" followed by, "How do electric car engines work?" and then, "What are the benefits of using electric cars over gasoline cars?" This method helps maintain a clear and structured flow of information, especially when tackling intricate topics or when you need to understand a subject deeply.

Creativity in Prompt Design

Incorporating creativity in your prompts can lead to surprisingly delightful and insightful interactions with ChatGPT. This involves thinking outside the box and asking questions that push the boundaries of the usual interactions. For example, instead of asking, "What are the health benefits of walking?" you might phrase your prompt as, "Imagine walking is a new product. What would be its advertising tagline based on its health benefits?" Such creative prompts encourage ChatGPT to tap into its training on diverse data sets, often leading to unique, clever, and entertaining responses that might provide new perspectives on familiar topics.

Leveraging Known Parameters

Incorporating known parameters into your prompts can significantly enhance the specificity and relevance of the responses from ChatGPT. This technique involves using specific data points you already know to inform the AI's response process. For instance, if you are a small business owner looking to increase local traffic to your store, a prompt like, "What are effective marketing strategies for a small business in Boston with a limited budget?" helps ChatGPT understand your query's geographical and financial context. By grounding your prompt with these known parameters, you direct ChatGPT to tailor its computational prowess to your specific situation, making the advice or information it provides more applicable and actionable.

As you experiment with these advanced prompting techniques, you'll discover that how you ask questions can dramatically influence the quality and applicability of the answers you receive. This realization is a powerful aspect of learning to interact effectively with AI. It highlights the importance of clear, thoughtful communication and shows how creativity and precision can unlock the full potential of ChatGPT and similar tools. As you continue to practice and refine your prompting skills, remember that each interaction is an opportunity to enhance your understanding and mastery of this dynamic interface between human curiosity and artificial intelligence.

2.3 Troubleshooting Common Prompting Errors

Navigating the nuances of prompt engineering can sometimes feel like steering a ship through uncharted waters—there are moments when things don't go exactly as planned. Understanding how to identify and correct common prompting errors is like having a reliable compass; it ensures that you can recalibrate and steer back to a course of productive and insightful interactions with ChatGPT. Let's delve into some common challenges you might encounter and explore strategies to overcome them effectively.

Diagnosing Vague Responses

At times, you may find that ChatGPT's responses seem vague or barely touch on the topic you're interested in. This often happens when the prompt lacks specific guiding elements that help narrow the AI's focus. To tackle this, revise your prompt to include more detailed information about what you want to know or achieve. For instance, if your initial question was "Tell me about renewable energy," and you received a generic overview, you could specify your interest by changing it to "What are the latest advancements in solar energy technology in Europe?" This refined prompt provides clear direction, encouraging ChatGPT to generate a more targeted and detailed response. Additionally, incorporating follow-up questions based on the initial answers can help dig deeper into the subject, like peeling an onion layer by layer to reveal more substantive information with each query.

Correcting Over-Specificity

While specificity is usually beneficial, overly detailed prompts can sometimes limit the breadth of ChatGPT's responses, confining it to a narrow scope that might miss other valuable insights. For example, if you ask, "What is the average price of a 256GB iPhone 12 in New York City?" you might restrict the response to very specific data that may not be readily available or useful. To find a balance, consider broadening your prompt to capture a wider range of information while guiding the AI toward your specific interest area. A better approach could be, "How do iPhone prices vary across different models and storage capacities in major US cities?" This revised prompt invites a more comprehensive discussion, which can be more informative and useful.

Handling Non-Responses and Errors

Occasionally, you might encounter situations where ChatGPT fails to respond or returns an error. This can happen for various reasons, such as network issues, overly complex queries, or AI training data limitations. When this occurs, the first step is simplifying your prompt to streamline the AI process. Breaking down a complex question into smaller, more manageable parts can help avoid overwhelming the system. Additionally, ensuring that your internet connection is stable and that the platform hosting ChatGPT is operational can resolve some of these issues. If errors persist, it's helpful to report them to the service provider, as this can aid in improving the system for all users.

Feedback Mechanisms

One of the most effective ways to refine your prompts and enhance the quality of interactions with ChatGPT is to utilize feedback mechanisms. Every response from the AI offers insights into how well it understood and addressed your query. You can adjust your prompting strategy to achieve better results by critically analyzing these responses. For instance, if a response misses key points you hoped to cover, consider rephrasing your prompt to highlight these areas more clearly in your next interaction. Additionally, some platforms allow users to rate or provide feedback on AI responses directly, which can help improve the system's accuracy and responsiveness over time.

Mastering these troubleshooting techniques requires patience and practice but is undoubtedly rewarding. As you become more adept at identifying and correcting prompting errors, your interactions with ChatGPT will become more fluid, productive, and enlightening. Just like any skill, prompt engineering improves with experience, and each challenge you overcome adds a layer of proficiency, enhancing your ability to harness the full potential of this powerful conversational AI.

2.4 Using Prompts to Generate Creative Content

When exploring the capabilities of ChatGPT, one particularly exciting application is its ability to aid in creative endeavors. Whether you're a writer, an artist, or someone just looking to explore your creative side, learning how to craft prompts that encourage creative outputs from ChatGPT can open up a world of possibilities. Let's jump into how this tool can inspire your artistic expressions, enhance storytelling, and even solve problems creatively.

Inspiring Artistic Expressions

Imagine you're looking to write a poem but are stuck for inspiration. ChatGPT can serve as a collaborative partner in your creative process. Start by setting a theme or emotion you want to explore in your poem and use a prompt to guide ChatGPT. For instance, you could say, "Write a poem about the tranquility of the ocean at dusk." ChatGPT will generate a poem that adheres to your theme and introduces unique perspectives and word choices you might not have considered. Similarly, if you're an artist looking for ideas for your next painting, you might prompt ChatGPT with, "Describe a scene that combines elements of surrealism and nature." The response could spark a vision of a landscape that defies the ordinary, fueling your artistic imagination.

Brainstorming with AI

ChatGPT can also be an invaluable tool for brainstorming. Whether you're looking to develop new project ideas, find solutions to business challenges, or think of topics for academic research, the way you frame your prompts can lead to a wealth of innovative ideas. Suppose you're tasked with developing a new product idea for a fitness technology company. You could use a prompt like, "List innovative features that could be included in a fitness tracker to enhance user engagement." ChatGPT might suggest features you hadn't thought of, such as stress level detection or integration with virtual reality for immersive workouts, each of which could serve as a starting point for further exploration.

Enhancing Storytelling

For writers and storytellers, crafting prompts that aid in developing complex narratives or character arcs is another area where ChatGPT can be particularly useful. If you're writing a story and are stuck on character development, you might ask, "Create a backstory for a character who is a retired astronaut turned detective." ChatGPT's response can provide a detailed past that adds depth to your character, enriching your narrative. Additionally, if you're looking to build a compelling plot twist, a prompt such as, "Suggest a plot twist for a mystery novel where the least likely character is the culprit" could provide you with unexpected ideas that enhance the intrigue and complexity of your story.

Creative Problem Solving

Finally, ChatGPT can assist in creative problem-solving by generating novel solutions to problems or offering new perspectives on existing situations. This capability is instrumental in marketing, product development, and personal challenges. For example, if you're trying to increase attendance at a local event, you might ask ChatGPT, "What are some creative marketing strategies to increase local engagement with a community event?" The suggestions might include innovative uses of social media, partnerships with local businesses, or interactive campaigns that engage potential attendees in a memorable way. Each idea can be evaluated and adapted to fit your needs and resources.

Harnessing ChatGPT for creative content generation involves a shift in how you approach problem-solving and idea development. You open up innovative possibilities by effectively leveraging AI's ability to process and generate text based on your prompts. Whether you're writing a novel, planning a marketing strategy, or simply exploring artistic expressions, ChatGPT can be a powerful ally in your creator toolkit. As you continue experimenting with different prompts and exploring the AI's potential, you'll likely discover that your creative skills are enhanced, leading to richer, more innovative outcomes in whatever project you undertake.

2.5 Ethical Considerations in Prompt Engineering

When engaging with tools like ChatGPT, it is important to remember and apply the foundational ethics discussed in Chapter One. These principles ensure that your prompts foster responsible and ethical AI use. Your prompts can significantly influence the outputs, so avoiding creating or sharing manipulative or harmful content is crucial. Instead, focus on generating prompts that encourage positive, constructive, and unbiased responses. For example, if you're exploring sensitive topics like mental health or social issues, frame your prompts thoughtfully to respect the complexity of these subjects and avoid perpetuating stereotypes or biases.

Bias and fairness are significant concerns in AI that can be influenced by how prompts are designed. AI systems like ChatGPT learn from vast datasets that may contain biased human language or perspectives. These biases can be reflected in the AI's responses. To counteract this, ensure your prompts are neutral and avoid assumptions about personal characteristics like race, gender, or age unless relevant to the context. Diversifying the scenarios and examples in your prompts can also help provide a broader perspective and reduce the prevalence of narrow or stereotypical responses. For instance, when asking about leadership, consider including various cultural, social, and organizational contexts to enrich the diversity of responses. Effective prompting can help alleviate bias by explicitly requesting balanced perspectives and inclusive considerations, thereby guiding ChatGPT to generate more equitable responses that reflect diverse viewpoints.

Privacy is another critical consideration when using AI. Although ChatGPT does not retain personal data for future interactions, it is essential to be cautious with the information you include in your prompts. Avoid sharing personal details or confidential information, particularly if the outputs will be shared or are accessible to others. Additionally, when generating content, ensure that personal data or identifiable details are fictionalized to prevent privacy breaches. This helps maintain the integrity of your data and protects sensitive information from misuse. Remember that your prompts may be used to help train and improve the AI, so always consider the potential implications of the information you provide. This approach helps maintain the integrity of your data and protects sensitive information from misuse.

Transparency is key when utilizing AI for content creation. As AI-generated content can be highly sophisticated, it is important to be honest about the use of AI in generating responses. Disclose AI involvement in your content creation process, especially in contexts where authenticity and credibility are important, such as academic or journalistic work. For example, if you use ChatGPT to help draft articles or reports, include a note that acknowledges the role of AI. This transparency upholds ethical standards and fosters trust and critical engagement with your audience.

By considering these ethical considerations, you can ensure that your prompt engineering is both responsible and beneficial. Focus on creating prompts reflecting fairness and respect for privacy while maintaining transparent disclosure procedures. This approach enhances the quality and integrity of your interactions with AI, aligns with broader ethical values, and contributes positively to the responsible development and use of AI technologies.

2.6 Customizing Prompts for Niche Topics

In the expansive terrain of AI applications, the ability to tailor ChatGPT's responses to specific industry needs or cultural contexts greatly enhances its utility and relevance. This customization is not just about refining the tool's accuracy; it's about molding it to become a seamless extension of your environment, whether in a bustling hospital ward, a fast-paced financial trading floor, or a multicultural marketing firm. Let's explore sophisticated strategies to fine-tune your interactions with ChatGPT, ensuring it responds with the precision and appropriateness required by different professional and cultural landscapes.

Industry-Specific Prompts

Every industry has specific language, regulations, and unique scenarios requiring specialized knowledge. To make ChatGPT a valuable tool for your field, it's important to tailor your prompts to meet these industry-specific requirements. This approach transforms ChatGPT from a generalist into a specialized asset. For example, accuracy and up-to-date information are crucial in the legal field. A prompt like "Explain the implications of the latest amendment in the data protection law for tech companies" must elicit a response that understands legal terms and reflects current laws and practices. Similarly, it's vital to ensure that prompts lead to medically accurate and confidential responses in healthcare. Asking, "What are the recommended treatments for type 2 diabetes according to the latest medical research?" should provide answers based on the most recent medical standards and research. In finance, where data changes rapidly, prompts must reflect the latest trends and information. A query like "Analyze the trend in tech stocks over the last quarter" requires the AI to understand and accurately interpret current financial data. Crafting such prompts involves knowing the specific needs of your industry and expressing them clearly in your questions to ChatGPT. This ensures that the responses you receive are relevant, accurate, and timely, making ChatGPT a more effective tool for your professional use.

Cultural Sensitivity

As businesses and interactions increasingly cross borders, the ability to customize prompts for cultural relevance and sensitivity becomes crucial. This involves understanding and integrating cultural nuances that affect communication styles, preferences, and taboos. For instance, when dealing with markets or audiences in different regions, the tone, examples, and references should be adapted to resonate culturally. A prompt intended for an audience in Japan, such as "Suggest polite marketing phrases for elderly customers," should reflect the formal and respectful communication style prevalent in Japanese culture. Similarly, a content creation prompt for a Middle Eastern audience should be aware of cultural norms and local tastes to ensure the content is engaging and appropriate. This customization enhances the effectiveness of the communication and builds a respectful and inclusive interaction framework.

Experimental Uses

The flexibility of ChatGPT opens up a playground for experimental applications. Encouraging experimentation with prompts can lead to innovative uses that push the boundaries of what AI can achieve. For instance, experimenting with ChatGPT in artistic domains, such as co-writing scripts for plays or generating ideas for art installations, can yield creative synergies that were previously unexplored. Similarly, in education, prompts can be designed to create interactive learning experiences that adapt to different learning styles and paces. Such experimental applications showcase the versatility of ChatGPT but also inspire continuous improvement and adaptation in various fields.

Embracing these advanced strategies for customizing ChatGPT's responses ensures that the tool is not just a passive participant in your tasks but dynamically tuned to the specific frequencies of your professional and cultural environment. Whether through industry-specific adjustments, cultural fine-tuning, or innovative experimentations, the potential to mold ChatGPT to fit almost any niche is immense. As you continue to interact and refine these approaches, the depth and breadth of ChatGPT's utility will only expand, mirroring the complexity and diversity of the human interactions it seeks to emulate.

2.7 The Perfect Prompt Formula

Crafting the perfect prompt for ChatGPT is akin to composing a recipe that balances all ingredients to achieve a delightful dish. Just as chefs use precise measurements and specific techniques to enhance flavors, effective prompts require a mix of clarity, context, and creativity to elicit the best responses. Let's explore how you can create clear, contextually rich, targeted prompts to yield precise and useful outcomes from ChatGPT.

Task Specification

Starting your prompt with a precise action verb is crucial as it sets the direction for ChatGPT, specifying what you expect as an outcome. This approach is similar to giving a clear command that guides someone on what to do next. For instance, a prompt like "Summarize the main points of this article" uses the action verb 'summarize' to direct ChatGPT to condense the article into its key elements. Similarly, "Create a detailed outline for a blog post on healthy eating," tells ChatGPT to 'create' something and specifies that it should be a 'detailed outline,' which narrows down the form of the response. These examples show that starting with a specific action verb can significantly streamline the interaction, making it easier for ChatGPT to understand and fulfill the request effectively.

Context Provision

Including relevant background details or situational context in your prompts enhances ChatGPT's understanding and the appropriateness of its responses. This is like setting the scene in a play; the better the scene is set, the more accurate the performance. For example, when you use a prompt like "Considering the current market trends, explain the benefits of this new product," you're not only asking for a task (explain) but also framing it within the specific context of "current market trends." This leads ChatGPT to tailor its response to how the new product fits or stands out in the current market scenario. Similarly, "In the context of an entry-level job interview, draft a cover letter for a marketing position" provides a clear scenario, helping ChatGPT focus its response to match the formality and specifics expected in a specific scenario.

Example Inclusion

You guide ChatGPT on the expected response style by incorporating examples into your prompts. This technique ensures that the output aligns closely with your needs. For instance, a prompt such as "Write the cover letter using the format pasted here [paste example]" clearly shows how the response should be structured. This makes it easier for ChatGPT to generate the desired content and ensures that the final output meets your requirements. Similarly, "Create a list of pros and cons, such as: 'Pros: Affordable, Easy to use; Cons: Limited features,'" clearly dictates both the content and the format, making the response immediately usable. Examples aren't always necessary, but they provide an excellent guide when used.

Persona Adoption

Specifying a persona in your prompts can significantly influence ChatGPT's responses, tailoring them to suit your intended audience better. Although this step is optional, it can be particularly helpful when you need precise and context-specific answers. For example, prompting, "You are a data analyst for a retail company considering a new job," helps ChatGPT adopt a relevant domain and provide clear, focused insights. Similarly, specifying constraints like, "You only have two hours each day," guides ChatGPT in offering practical solutions within the given time frame. This strategy ensures the responses are accurate in content and framed from the appropriate perspective.

Format Specification

Specifying the preferred structure for a response can greatly improve the organization and usability of the information you receive. Whether you need a list or a detailed paragraph, clearly stating the desired format helps ensure the response meets your needs. For instance, you can ask ChatGPT to "List the key points" or "List the steps" in bullet format for a concise and easy-to-scan list or to "Write a paragraph summarizing the benefits" for a more detailed narrative. This clarity in formatting instructions ensures the output aligns with your intended use, whether for a presentation, report, or casual reading. You might also provide detailed instructions like "use markdown formatting with ### for main headings, #### for subheadings, bullet points (-), and numbered lists (1., 2., 3.)." This approach helps you receive well-organized information tailored to your specific requirements.

Tone Indication

Finally, specifying the tone and style of the response is crucial for ensuring that the communication is adequate and appropriate for the context. For example, "Use a friendly and conversational tone" for a blog post aimed at young adults helps make the content relatable and engaging. In contrast, "Draft the email in a formal and professional manner" is appropriate for correspondence in a business context, where a higher level of formality is expected. This attention to tone and style enhances the effectiveness of the communication and reflects your understanding and respect for the audience's expectations.

Mastering the art of prompt crafting using these elements ensures that every interaction with ChatGPT is productive, targeted, and aligned with your objectives. As you practice incorporating these elements into your prompts, you'll find that ChatGPT has become an increasingly powerful tool, capable of generating precise and useful content that can save you time and enhance your projects or communications.

2.8 Interactive Task: Perfecting Your Prompting Skills

Engaging with ChatGPT is akin to learning a new language; the more you practice, the more fluent you become. To enhance your prompting skills, it's essential to immerse yourself in varied and structured practice exercises. These exercises are designed to gradually increase your comfort and proficiency by creating effective prompts tailored to elicit the best responses from ChatGPT.

Prompt Refinement and Improvement

Let's start with a foundational exercise to build your prompting skills. Begin by choosing a topic you're curious about, such as "sustainable gardening." First, formulate a basic prompt: "Tell me about sustainable gardening." Analyze the response from ChatGPT for completeness and relevance. Next, refine your prompt to make it more specific: "What are five sustainable gardening practices that can be easily implemented at home?" Notice how the specificity of your prompt enhances the precision of the response. Continue this exercise by gradually increasing the complexity of your prompts, such as asking for the pros and cons of each practice mentioned. This step-by-step escalation not only hones your ability to ask straightforward, focused questions but also deepens your understanding of the topic.

Progressive Prompting

Let's enhance your prompting skills by building upon each response in progressive queries. Imagine you are helping a friend start a small online business. Begin with a general prompt to gather foundational information, such as, "What are the key elements of a digital business plan?" Once ChatGPT provides a response, analyze the data and think about the next logical step to delve deeper into the topic. For example, follow up with a more focused question, "Can you explain how to identify and analyze target markets for an online business?" After receiving this detailed response, continue building on this by asking, "What strategies can be used to market an online business to these identified target markets effectively?" This step-by-step approach sharpens your ability to create precise prompts and demonstrates how to build on each piece of information provided by ChatGPT. It mimics a natural and progressive topic exploration, enabling you to extract comprehensive insights and progressively more detailed information.

Crafting the Perfect Prompt

Choose a topic (e.g., "healthy eating" or "time management) and a specific situation in which you're interested. Use the Perfect Prompt Formula to craft your prompt by specifying the task, providing context, including an example, adopting a persona, specifying the format, and indicating the tone. This exercise will help you practice creating effective prompts that generate accurate and tailored responses from ChatGPT.

You are on the right track if your prompt looked something like this: "You recently secured a new position as a data analyst. Your friends, impressed by your determination and strategy, have asked for your advice on their own job searches. Write a message in paragraph form to share with your friends seeking new job opportunities in a group chat. The message should outline the key steps you took in your job search, share some challenges you faced and how you overcame them, and offer to support them as they embark on their own job searches. Use motivational and supportive language." Continue practicing with the Perfect Prompt Formula, either with new topics or by refining existing ones, until you are comfortable crafting "perfect" prompts. Try different scenarios and progressively more complex situations to enhance your skills and confidence in prompt crafting.

Through these exercises, you'll notice a significant improvement in your communication ability with ChatGPT. Each step, from simple questions to complex, scenario-based prompts, incrementally builds your skill and confidence. Remember, every prompt is a chance to refine your approach, expand your knowledge, and enhance your interaction with this advanced AI, making each exchange more valuable and insightful.

As we conclude this chapter on honing your prompting skills, remember that clear communication is the key to successful interactions. This includes defining your task, setting the context, providing examples, adopting the right persona, and specifying the format and tone. These elements combine to form a formula that enhances the efficiency and effectiveness of your prompts. Looking ahead, the next chapter will build on these skills, showing you how to fully apply them in real-world scenarios to utilize ChatGPT in various professional contexts. Stay tuned to continue refining your skills and discover how to leverage ChatGPT to enhance business productivity, streamline daily tasks, and support your professional growth and development.

Business Productivity with ChatGPT

Welcome to Chapter Three! Building on the prompt engineering skills you've developed, we will now progress into how you can use ChatGPT to enhance business productivity. This chapter will guide you through various applications to streamline your work, manage tasks more efficiently, and support your professional development.

Envision a world where your daily business communications are faster, more efficient, personalized, and engaging. This isn't a glimpse into a far-off future; it's a reality you can achieve today with the power of ChatGPT. This chapter discusses how ChatGPT can transform your approach to essential business tasks such as writing emails, creating content, and managing customer service inquiries. You'll also explore how ChatGPT can assist in educational endeavors, solve business problems, and take on personal assistant duties. From managing your social media to conducting market research, ChatGPT's capabilities will help you enhance every aspect of your professional life. Get ready to unlock new levels of productivity and efficiency with practical applications and real-world examples that illustrate the transformative power of AI in your daily work.

3.1 Enhancing Emails with ChatGPT

Drafting Routine Responses

One of the significant benefits of integrating ChatGPT into your email work-flow is its ability to help draft routine responses efficiently. Businesses often receive repetitive inquiries, such as questions about business hours or return policies. Crafting each response manually can be a significant time drain. While ChatGPT cannot send emails for you, it can be used to draft accurate and consistent replies quickly. For example, you can instruct ChatGPT to generate a response for inquiries about return policies by providing a standard template or key points. This helps ensure your replies are consistent and professional, reflecting your business's values and saving you time to focus on more person-alized interactions.

Organizing and Summarizing Emails

Managing a high volume of incoming emails can be overwhelming, but Chat-GPT can assist by helping you organize and prioritize them more effectively. One way to utilize ChatGPT is by exporting the contents of your mailbox and using it in a prompt to create a prioritization summary. This lets you quickly identify which emails require immediate attention and which can be deferred. Additionally, you can use the export to generate concise summaries of the content, providing quick insights into the key points without reading through each email in detail. Furthermore, prompting ChatGPT to analyze the exported emails can help identify potential business processes that could improve your workflow. While ChatGPT does not manage your inbox directly, leveraging it for summarizing and prioritizing email content can streamline your email management, ensuring that critical communications are highlighted and saving you significant time.

Personalizing Bulk Emails

Enhancing efficiency in email communication goes beyond drafting responses—it involves recognizing where personalization can make the most impact. ChatGPT can help you identify areas within your emails that are prime for personalization by analyzing customer data, such as past purchases and interactions. For instance, by reviewing the contents of your email exports, ChatGPT can highlight segments that would benefit from tailored messages, ensuring that each communication feels individualized and thoughtful rather than generic. This is particularly useful for bulk communications, such as promotional campaigns, where personalized recommendations based on customer preferences can significantly improve engagement and satisfaction. While ChatGPT will not personalize the emails for you, it can pinpoint opportunities where personalization will be most effective, allowing you to craft content that enhances customer loyalty and trust manually.

Enhancing Email Creativity

Maintaining creativity in email communications can be challenging, especially when dealing with routine business tasks. ChatGPT, with its vast training data covering various writing styles, can help you draft emails that are not only clear and effective but also engaging and creative. For example, if you are preparing a newsletter or a promotional email, ChatGPT can suggest compelling language for subject lines, calls to action, and content that resonates with your audience. This helps make your emails more attractive and can lead to higher engagement rates, particularly useful for marketing and outreach efforts.

Integrating ChatGPT into your email management routine can significantly improve your efficiency and the quality of your communications. You can save time and increase productivity by using ChatGPT to draft routine responses, organize incoming emails, personalize emails, and enhance communication creativity. As you continue exploring the capabilities of ChatGPT in this chapter, you will discover even more practical ways to streamline your business tasks and improve your overall work efficiency.

3.2 Streamlining Content Creation

Creating content consistently can be daunting, especially when you are expected to keep high-quality and fresh ideas. ChatGPT can significantly streamline this process by assisting in several key areas, from generating topic ideas to structuring content and optimizing it for better search engine visibility. Let's explore leveraging Chat GPT to make content creation more efficient and impactful.

Generating Ideas and Outlines

Every great piece of writing starts with a solid idea and a clear outline, and this is where ChatGPT can be incredibly useful. Suppose you want to write about psychology but are unsure what angle to take. By inputting "general terms related to psychology" into ChatGPT, you can generate a list of potential topics such as 'Cognition,' 'Emotion,' or 'Social Psychology.' Each of these topics can serve as a springboard for more detailed articles. Once a topic is selected, ChatGPT can help you create a structured outline. For instance, if you choose 'Forensic Psychology,' ChatGPT can suggest key sections for the article and prompt Chat GPT to draft an outline for the selected focus area. This structured approach saves time, sparks new ideas, and guides you toward a more thoughtful and comprehensive topic exploration.

Drafting Content

With a robust outline in place, the next step is drafting the content. ChatGPT can serve as a first-pass writer, generating drafts based on the outlines provided. This doesn't mean it will replace your unique voice or style, but it gives a solid base of text that you can refine and edit. For an article on forensic psychology, ChatGPT can elaborate on each section of the outline with relevant information, forming paragraphs that explain the concepts in a straightforward manner. This draft can be enhanced with your insights, additional research, and stylistic adjustments. This process significantly reduces the time you would spend on writing initial drafts and allows you to focus more on adding value through your expertise and unique perspective.

Improving SEO

In the digital age, just writing good content isn't enough; your content must also be optimized for search engines to reach a wider audience. ChatGPT can assist by integrating SEO best practices into your content creation workflow. It can suggest relevant keywords likely to increase your content's visibility. For example, for the forensic psychology article, ChatGPT can identify high-impact keywords such as Criminal Behavior Analysis,' 'Crime Scene Analysis,' or 'Insanity Defense.' Furthermore, ChatGPT can help you naturally incorporate these keywords into the article, enhancing readability and SEO without resorting to keyword stuffing, which can detract from the quality of the writing. Additionally, Chat GPT can suggest meta descriptions and tags optimized for search engines, ensuring that your content is informative and more likely to be discovered by those interested in the topic.

Content Scaling

Scaling content production without compromising quality is a critical challenge for marketers and creators. ChatGPT is particularly beneficial in this regard. By automating the initial stages of content creation - from ideation to drafting - ChatGPT allows you to produce more content in less time. This is especially useful for businesses looking to maintain a robust online presence with a steady stream of fresh content. Moreover, because ChatGPT handles the foundational aspects of writing, you can allocate more resources to enhancing the content through multimedia additions, interactive elements, and detailed research, thereby increasing your articles' overall value and appeal. This ability to scale content efficiently helps keep your blog or website dynamic and engaging and supports your audience growth and engagement goals.

Integrating ChatGPT into your content creation process transforms the way you produce content. From the initial brainstorming to the final touches that prepare a piece for publication, ChatGPT is a versatile tool that saves time, boosts productivity, and enhances the quality of your content. As you continue to leverage this technology, you'll find that you can meet and exceed the demands of your content-creating schedule, allowing you the freedom to focus on creative and strategic endeavors that further your publication's success.

3.3 Leveraging ChatGPT for Customer Service Efficiency

In the fast-paced realm of customer service, responsiveness and efficiency are key. Integrating ChatGPT into your customer service operations can revolutionize how you manage inquiries, ensuring that each customer feels heard and valued from the moment they reach out. While ChatGPT cannot respond to customers automatically, it can assist you by drafting accurate and helpful responses, suggesting solutions based on historical data, and providing multilingual support to help address inquiries in different languages. Additionally, ChatGPT can integrate with some Customer Relationship Management (CRM) systems to analyze past interactions, highlight common issues, and recommend personalized responses, making it an invaluable asset for enhancing customer service efficiency and effectiveness.

Response Drafting and Multilingual Assistance

ChatGPT can play a significant supportive role in customer service by drafting accurate and helpful responses. When customer service representatives receive inquiries, ChatGPT can quickly generate initial response drafts, saving valuable time and ensuring consistency in communication. This allows representatives to focus on fine-tuning responses to meet specific customer needs rather than starting from scratch. Moreover, ChatGPT excels in providing multilingual support, which is crucial in today's globalized business environment. It can assist in crafting responses in various languages, helping your team effectively address a diverse customer base. ChatGPT ensures that customers from different regions feel understood and valued by facilitating communication across language barriers, enhancing their overall experience with your brand. This capability improves response efficiency and broadens customer service reach, providing more inclusive and comprehensive support.

Data Analysis and CRM Integration

ChatGPT enhances customer service efficiency by leveraging data analysis and integrating seamlessly with CRM systems. By analyzing past interactions and customer data stored within your CRM, ChatGPT can identify common issues and recurring patterns, providing valuable insights that inform your customer service strategies. This can help prepare preemptive responses to frequently encountered problems, saving time and improving service quality. To connect ChatGPT with your CRM system, you may need assistance from your technical team to set up the integration, which is typically done through an API. Once connected, ChatGPT can suggest contextually relevant responses based on a customer's history, ensuring timely and highly personalized replies. This integration reduces the time needed to resolve inquiries and enhances the effectiveness of your customer service operations, leading to quicker and more satisfactory resolutions for your customers.

Personalization and Recommendation Capabilities

ChatGPT's ability to personalize interactions and provide tailored recommendations significantly enhances the quality of customer service. By analyzing customer data such as purchase history, preferences, and past interactions, ChatGPT can suggest personalized responses that resonate more deeply with individual customers. This level of personalization ensures that each customer feels valued and understood, as their specific needs and concerns are addressed directly. For example, if a customer has previously inquired about a product, ChatGPT can craft a response that references their previous interaction, providing a sense of continuity and attentiveness. Additionally, ChatGPT can recommend products, services, or solutions that align with the customer's interests and previous behaviors, fostering a more engaging and relevant dialogue. These personalized recommendations enhance customer satisfaction and encourage loyalty and repeat business, as customers are more likely to return when a company consistently meets their needs. This capability to provide bespoke advice and solutions helps differentiate your service from generic customer support, creating a more meaningful and productive customer experience.

Integrating ChatGPT into your customer service operations offers a multifaceted approach to enhancing efficiency, personalization, and overall customer satisfaction. By supporting the drafting of accurate responses and providing multilingual assistance, ChatGPT helps streamline communication and broadens your ability to effectively serve a diverse customer base. Its ability to analyze and integrate data with CRM systems allows for identifying common issues, enabling more proactive and informed customer service strategies. Furthermore, ChatGPT's capability to personalize responses and offer tailored recommendations creates a more engaging and relevant customer experience, fostering greater loyalty and satisfaction. By leveraging these advanced features, ChatGPT reduces your workload and ensures that each interaction has the level of care and attention customers desire. As you refine your use of ChatGPT, you'll find that it becomes an invaluable tool in delivering responsive, efficient, and personalized customer service, setting your business apart in today's competitive market.

3.4 ChatGPT in Education: Aiding Learning and Research

In the realm of education, ChatGPT offers a wealth of opportunities to enhance learning. Rather than serving as a shortcut for completing assignments, ChatGPT is a powerful resource that can help learners explore topics in-depth, develop critical thinking skills, and find additional explanations or perspectives on complex subjects. It is a versatile educational tool that can provide guidance, generate ideas for research projects, assist with language learning, and even help students practice problem-solving. This section shows how ChatGPT can complement and enhance traditional learning techniques, making education more efficient and enriching while firmly upholding academic integrity. By leveraging ChatGPT responsibly, students and educators can foster a more supportive and honest learning environment that promotes genuine understanding and educational growth.

Tutoring and Homework Help

Imagine having a tutor available at any hour of the day, ready to assist with any question from various subjects. ChatGPT can be that tutor. For students, whether grappling with complex algebra problems or needing clarification on historical events, ChatGPT acts like a knowledgeable friend who is always there to help. Its ability to provide detailed, step-by-step explanations can make learning more accessible and less stressful. For example, suppose you're struggling with a math problem. In that case, ChatGPT can break down the solution process into comprehensible steps, ensuring you not only get the correct answer but understand the how and why behind it. This capability is not just about providing answers; it's about enhancing understanding and fostering a deeper interest in learning.

Furthermore, for subjects that require essay writing, ChatGPT can assist in structuring your arguments or providing feedback on drafts. You could input your essay draft and ask ChatGPT to suggest improvements or identify areas where your arguments need strengthening. This interactive form of learning improves academic skills and encourages critical thinking and self-reflection, essential skills in any educational journey.

Research Assistance

The initial stages of gathering information for a project or paper can be daunting for students and researchers. ChatGPT can simplify this process by helping to compile preliminary data and sources. If you're starting a research project, you can ask ChatGPT for the latest studies or articles on your topic. For instance, if your research pertains to environmental science, ChatGPT can summarize recent research papers on climate change, including authors, key findings, and publication dates. This speeds up the research process and ensures you have a solid foundation of up-to-date information before diving deeper into specialized databases or academic journals.

Moreover, ChatGPT's ability to filter and prioritize information based on your specific needs can be incredibly beneficial. It can aggregate this information if you need data from multiple sources, providing a comprehensive overview highlighting major themes and gaps in the existing research. This level of customized assistance is akin to having a research assistant available at any moment to support your academic endeavors, making the research process more efficient and enjoyable.

Interactive Learning

The traditional education model often involves passive learning, where students sometimes listen to lectures and read material without much engagement. ChatGPT can transform this dynamic by creating interactive learning experiences that make education more engaging and effective. Through simulations or role-playing exercises, ChatGPT can bring theoretical concepts to life. For example, in a business class, ChatGPT could simulate a negotiation scenario between two companies, requiring the student to make decisions based on economic principles. This method helps students apply theoretical knowledge in practical situations, enhancing their understanding and retention of complex concepts.

Another powerful application of ChatGPT is in language learning. ChatGPT can engage students in conversations in the language they are learning, offering immediate feedback and ample practice opportunities essential for language acquisition. This interactive approach mimics real-life discussions, allowing students to practice and refine their language skills in a dynamic and engaging way that traditional classroom settings may not fully replicate. For instance, a prompt like "Describe your day in Spanish" encourages students to practice their language skills in a natural context, enhancing their conversational abilities and fostering greater fluency. ChatGPT helps learners build confidence and proficiency in using the language in everyday scenarios by providing a simulated conversational partner.

Assessment Preparation

Preparing for exams can be stressful for students, but ChatGPT can ease this process by generating practice questions and topics for revision. If you're preparing for a biology exam, ChatGPT can create a series of potential exam questions based on the syllabus, ranging from multiple-choice questions to more complex essay questions. This helps you anticipate the types of questions you might encounter and provides a structured way to test your knowledge and identify areas where you might need further study.

Additionally, ChatGPT can help organize revision notes, summarizing key points from your textbooks or lecture notes into concise, easy-to-review documents. This can be particularly helpful for visual learners who benefit from clear, organized materials. By providing a variety of ways to review and test your knowledge, ChatGPT can make exam preparation less daunting, boosting your confidence and readiness to tackle any academic challenge. For other assessments, such as job interviews, Chat GPT can generate questions based on a job description and provide feedback on your responses.

Through these applications, ChatGPT stands out as a versatile tool in the educational landscape, capable of transforming how learning is approached. From personalized tutoring sessions and research assistance to creating engaging interactive learning experiences and aiding in exam preparation, ChatGPT empowers students to take control of their educational journey, making learning more effective and inspiring.

3.5 Personal Assistant Duties Handled by ChatGPT

Managing time efficiently is one of the most universally endorsed pathways to success and personal satisfaction in the bustling business and daily life. Imagine having a virtual assistant that helps keep your calendar in impeccable order, manages your travel itineraries, and prepares you for upcoming meetings—all with a few text prompts. This scenario isn't just a figment of the future; it's a present-day reality with ChatGPT. Let's delve into how this versatile AI can function as your personal assistant, streamlining tasks that traditionally consume a significant chunk of your day.

Scheduling and Calendars

Managing your schedule effectively can significantly enhance your productivity and reduce stress. ChatGPT can help you organize your schedule in several practical ways, making it easier to keep track of your commitments and plan your time efficiently. One of the most useful ways ChatGPT can assist you is by helping you generate a comprehensive schedule for the week or month. You can input your key activities and appointments, and ChatGPT can help you visualize them in an organized format. For example, you might ask, "Help me create a weekly schedule with my work meetings, gym sessions, and family commitments." ChatGPT can provide a structured layout to follow or transfer to your calendar easily.

Prioritizing Your Day

ChatGPT can help you plan your day by helping you prioritize tasks based on importance and urgency. You can list your tasks, and ChatGPT can suggest a sensible sequence. For instance, you might say, "I have five tasks to complete today. Can you help me prioritize them?" ChatGPT can help you decide which tasks to tackle first and how to allocate your time effectively.

Finding Time for New Activities

If you're looking to add new activities to your schedule, ChatGPT can help you find the best times for them. Whether you want to start a new hobby, fit in a workout, or schedule regular study sessions, ChatGPT can suggest optimal time slots based on your existing commitments. You can ask, "Can you suggest a time for me to jog three times a week?" ChatGPT will consider your current schedule and recommend times that fit your routine. ChatGPT can also help you determine the time it takes to tackle new hobbies if you are unsure about the time commitment.

Setting Up Routine Activities

For routine activities such as daily exercises, weekly shopping, or regular meetings, ChatGPT can help you establish a consistent schedule. Setting up these recurring tasks ensures that important activities become a regular part of your routine without remembering to schedule them each time. You can say, "Help me set a schedule for my weekly grocery shopping and daily meditation practice," and ChatGPT will suggest a regular time that fits into your overall schedule.

By leveraging ChatGPT to assist with these scheduling tasks, you can save time and ensure that your daily, weekly, and monthly activities are well-organized. This helps you stay on top of your commitments, avoid conflicts, and maintain a balanced schedule that supports your productivity and personal goals.

Travel Arrangements

Planning travel, whether for business or pleasure, involves many details that can be tedious to manage. ChatGPT can assist in making travel arrangements by researching flights, hotels, and even car rentals based on your preferences and budget. Suppose you need to attend a conference in another city. Simply inform ChatGPT of your travel dates and preferences, and it can handle the rest—from finding the best flights available to suggesting accommodations near the conference venue (The level of data recency will depend on the version of ChatGPT you are using). Additionally, ChatGPT can create detailed itineraries for your trips, including suggested activities and dining options based on online reviews and your past preferences. This level of assistance makes travel planning stress-free and allows you to focus on the purpose of your trip rather than the logistics.

Meeting Preparation

Preparing for meetings is more than just marking a date on your calendar. It often requires research, organization of materials, formulation of talking points, and understanding of possible rebuttals. ChatGPT can streamline these preparatory tasks by summarizing relevant documents and emails, thus ensuring you are well-informed about the discussion topics. If you're due to discuss a project update, ChatGPT can summarize the latest reports and progress and list key points for discussion. Moreover, it can help you draft content for presentations, documents needed for the meeting based on outlines or notes you provide, or simply help brainstorm ideas. This capability enhances your efficiency and boosts your confidence during sessions, as you are better prepared and informed.

Integrating ChatGPT into these aspects of your daily life streamlines your tasks. It frees up your time, allowing you to focus on strategic thinking, creativity, networking, or simply enjoying a less cluttered life. As businesses and lifestyles become increasingly complex, a tool like ChatGPT can significantly affect how efficiently and effectively you manage your responsibilities. Whether you're a busy professional looking to optimize your productivity or reduce your daily hustle, ChatGPT offers a range of functionalities that cater to a wide array of needs and preferences, making it an indispensable tool in the modern digital toolkit.

3.6 Personal Development using ChatGPT

In the ever-evolving landscape of personal development, continuous learning and goal-setting are pivotal elements that drive success and personal fulfillment. ChatGPT, with its advanced capabilities, is an invaluable tool to guide and support you in these endeavors. Whether you're looking to acquire new skills, set and track personal goals, or simply seek daily motivation, ChatGPT can be tailored to meet your specific needs, making the journey toward personal growth more manageable and engaging.

Skill Building

Imagine having access to a personal coach who guides you in learning new skills and recommends the best resources tailored to your learning style and goals. ChatGPT can fulfill this role by identifying and suggesting various resources, from online courses and informative books to interactive tutorials and learning content providers, that are aligned with your specific learning objectives. Suppose you're interested in learning digital marketing; ChatGPT can curate a list of the top-rated online courses, including detailed descriptions and user reviews, to help you make an informed decision. Additionally, it can suggest books that cover essential concepts and provide practical case studies for a deeper understanding of the subject.

Beyond recommending resources, ChatGPT can design personalized learning plans based on your schedule, learning pace, and progress. For instance, it can create a weekly study schedule that allocates time for watching tutorial videos, reading specific chapters from books, and completing online quizzes. This structured approach keeps your learning on track and makes the process less overwhelming, especially if you balance learning with other responsibilities. Furthermore, ChatGPT can track your progress by conducting quick recaps or quizzes at the end of each learning session, providing feedback on areas where you might need further review or practice. This ongoing assessment ensures that you are not just consuming information but are actively engaging and retaining knowledge.

Goal Setting and Tracking

Setting goals is a powerful practice to drive personal and professional growth, but the real challenge lies in consistently tracking and pursuing these goals. ChatGPT can assist you in setting realistic and achievable goals and breaking them down into manageable steps. For example, if your goal is to write a book, ChatGPT can help you outline the key milestones for the project, such as completing the outline, writing the first draft, and revising chapters. Each milestone can be assigned a timeline, making the goal less daunting and more structured.

You can also use ChatGPT to analyze your daily habits and routines, helping you identify the best practices to reach your goals. By inputting details about your daily activities, ChatGPT can help you evaluate which habits are most effective and which may need adjustment. For instance, you can describe your current routine, and ChatGPT can provide insights into how you might optimize your time, such as suggesting specific periods for focused work, exercise, or relaxation. This analysis can help you create a structured plan that aligns your daily actions with your long-term objectives. By focusing on positive habits and routines, ChatGPT can guide you towards consistent behaviors that lead to successful outcomes, ultimately enhancing your productivity and well-being.

Daily Motivation and Encouragement

Maintaining a positive mindset is crucial for personal growth and overall well-being. ChatGPT can contribute significantly by providing daily motivational quotes, affirmations, and encouraging words. Imagine starting your day by reading an inspiring quote or a positive affirmation from ChatGPT, setting a tone of optimism and motivation right from the morning. This can be particularly helpful during challenging times when your spirits are low, and you need a boost to keep going.

In addition to motivational messages, ChatGPT can provide personalized encouragement based on your recent activities or progress in your goals. If you've had a productive week, ChatGPT can acknowledge your efforts and encourage you to keep up the good work. Conversely, if you're facing setbacks, it can offer encouragement and remind you of your strengths and past accomplishments, helping you regain confidence and perspective. This tailored support not only enhances your emotional resilience but also fosters a mindset that is primed for growth and success.

Personal Journaling

Journaling is a powerful tool for self-reflection, allowing you to explore your thoughts, feelings, and experiences in a structured way. ChatGPT can enhance this practice by guiding journaling sessions with thought-provoking prompts and questions. Whether reflecting on a recent event, grappling with a decision, or simply documenting your day, ChatGPT can suggest prompts encouraging deep reflection and introspection. For example, ChatGPT might ask, "What were the key takeaways from your experience today?" or "How do you feel about the progress you've made on your goals this week?"

Additionally, ChatGPT can help organize your journal entries by categorizing them by themes or emotions, making it easier to track your personal growth over time. It can also analyze your entries to identify recurring patterns or themes, providing insights that might not be immediately obvious. For instance, if you frequently write about feeling stressed at work, ChatGPT can highlight this pattern, prompting you to explore coping strategies or consider changes to your work environment. This analytical aspect of journaling can be incredibly beneficial, as it helps you understand yourself better and make informed decisions that enhance your quality of life and personal satisfaction.

Leveraging ChatGPT for personal development gives you a versatile tool that supports your learning and goal-setting efforts, boosts your motivation, and aids in self-reflection. This multifaceted support makes the process of personal growth more manageable, enjoyable, and fulfilling. As you continue to explore and utilize these features, you'll likely discover even more ways ChatGPT can be customized to meet your unique needs and preferences, further enhancing your journey toward personal and professional fulfillment.

3.7 Interactive Task: Enhancing Business Productivity

Congratulations on completing Chapter Three! You've learned how ChatGPT can improve your business productivity, from enhancing email communications to streamlining content creation and customer service operations. Now, it's time to put these skills into practice with a hands-on task that will help reinforce what you've learned.

Instructions:

1. **Identify Your Needs:**

   - Reflect on your current business operations or daily tasks and identify areas where ChatGPT could improve efficiency. These could be routine email responses, generating content ideas, drafting customer service replies, or managing your schedule.

2. **Draft Prompts for Each Area:**

   - Write specific prompts using the perfect prompt formula to address each identified need.

3. **Test and Refine:**

   - Respond to each prompt and evaluate the output for accuracy, professionalism, and relevance.

   - Iterate over the output to get more accurate or helpful responses. This step is crucial for optimizing ChatGPT's efficiency in your workflow.

4. **Reflect and Share:**

- Reflect on your experience and consider how ChatGPT has changed your approach to business tasks.

- Share your insights and any tips you've discovered with colleagues, friends, or the AI community to help others enhance their productivity with ChatGPT.

As we conclude this chapter on enhancing business productivity, it's evident that ChatGPT is more than just a tool; it's a transformative addition to your daily workflow. The practical applications and benefits it offers demonstrate its versatility and impact. This hands-on task has equipped you with the knowledge to integrate ChatGPT into your work, helping you save time and improve efficiency. In the next chapter, we will explore how ChatGPT can enhance your life outside your workday and look at various ways this technology can assist you around the home in your leisure time.

Make a Difference with Your Review

Unlock the Power of Generosity

"We make a living by what we get. We make a life by what we give." - Winston Churchill

Hey there! People who give without expecting anything in return live longer, happier lives and even make more money. So, during our time together, let's give this a try.

I have a question for you...

Would you help someone you've never met, even if you never got credit for it?

Who is this person, you ask? They're just like you. Or, at least, like you used to be. They're less experienced, want to make a difference, and need help but are unsure where to look.

Our mission with this book is to make understanding ChatGPT accessible to everyone. Everything we do stems from that mission, and the only way for us to accomplish it is by reaching... everyone.

This is where you come in. Most people do, in fact, judge a book by its cover (and its reviews). So here's my ask on behalf of a struggling beginner you've never met:

Please help that beginner by leaving this book a review.

Your gift costs no money and takes less than 60 seconds to make real, but can change a fellow beginner's life forever. Your review could help...

- one more small business provide for their community.

- one more entrepreneur support their family.

- one more employee find meaningful work.

- one more client transform their life.

- one more dream come true.

To get that 'feel good' feeling and help this person for real, all you have to do is...and it takes less than 60 seconds...leave a review.

Simply click or scan the QR code below to leave your review:

If you feel good about helping a faceless beginner, you are my kind of person. Welcome to the club. You're one of us.

I'm even more excited to help you master ChatGPT faster and easier than you can possibly imagine. You'll love the lessons I'll share in the coming chapters.

Thank you from the bottom of my heart. Now, back to our regularly scheduled programming.

-Your biggest fan, The Rivanna Heights Media Team

P.S. Fun fact: If you provide something of value to another person, it makes you more valuable to them. If you believe this book will help someone you know, send this book their way.

ChatGPT for Your Personal Life

Welcome to Chapter Four, where we shift gears from professional productivity to the more personal and entertaining ways ChatGPT can enhance your daily life, smoothing your routines and making your leisure time more enjoyable. Think of transforming your mornings from chaotic or mundane into a series of uplifting and productive moments—this is not just wishful thinking but a tangible reality you can achieve with ChatGPT. Integrating this versatile AI into your morning routine can streamline how you start your day, ensuring you are well-informed, deeply motivated, and nutritionally satisfied before stepping out the door. Let's dive into how ChatGPT can become an integral part of your mornings, enhancing each start of your day with efficiency and positivity.

4.1 Morning Routines: Starting Your Day with ChatGPT

Motivational Quotes and Goals Review

Imagine starting your day not just with information but with inspiration. ChatGPT can be prompted to deliver daily motivational quotes that set a positive tone for your day. Additionally, it can remind you of your personal or professional goals to keep them in focus. You might ask ChatGPT, "Can you give me a motivational quote and remind me of my goals for today?" In response, ChatGPT could provide a quote such as, "Success is not final, failure is not fatal: It is the courage to continue that count." — Winston Churchill, followed by a reminder of your goals like, "Today, focus on completing the project proposal and remember to call your mentor for advice." This practice uplifts your spirits and aligns your daily activities with your long-term objectives, enhancing your immediate and ongoing motivation.

Breakfast Ideas and Recipes

Deciding what to eat for breakfast can sometimes be a hassle, especially when balancing nutrition with your busy schedule. ChatGPT can simplify this decision-making process by suggesting breakfast ideas and quick recipes based on your dietary preferences and what's available in your kitchen. You could say, "ChatGPT, I have eggs, spinach, and cheese. What can I make for breakfast quickly?" ChatGPT might suggest, "How about a spinach and cheese omelet? Here's a quick recipe: Beat 2 eggs, stir in chopped spinach and shredded cheese. Cook on a nonstick skillet over medium heat until the eggs are set and the cheese is melted. Serve hot." This personalized culinary assistance helps you prepare nutritious and enjoyable meals, ensuring you start your day with a satisfying and healthy breakfast.

Morning Meditation and Positive Affirmations

Embedding a mindfulness practice into your morning can profoundly impact your day's outlook and effectiveness. ChatGPT can guide you through short meditation sessions or generate positive affirmations to help center your thoughts and intentions for the day. You might ask, "ChatGPT, can you guide me through a five-minute meditation?" ChatGPT would then lead you through a calming sequence, perhaps instructing you to focus on breathing, recognize your body's presence, and release any tension. Following meditation, you could request, "Can you give me some positive affirmations for today?" ChatGPT could offer affirmations like, "I am confident in my ability to solve problems" or "I choose to focus on what I can control." Starting your day with meditation and affirmations can enhance your mental clarity and emotional resilience, setting a productive and positive tone for whatever lies ahead.

By integrating ChatGPT into your morning routine, you not only streamline how you start your day but also enhance the quality of your mornings, setting a precedent for productivity and positivity throughout the day. Whether through a tailored briefing, inspirational quotes, nutritious breakfast suggestions, or a centering meditation session, ChatGPT provides the tools and support necessary to transform your morning routine into a foundation for daily success and satisfaction. As you continue to explore and customize these interactions, you'll find that ChatGPT not only adapts to your lifestyle but also enriches it, making every morning a stepping stone to a fulfilled and accomplished day.

4.2 ChatGPT for Managing Personal Schedules

Managing your personal schedules effectively can be challenging in today's fast-paced world. However, integrating ChatGPT with your calendar apps can transform how you handle appointments and reminders, bringing efficiency and ease to your daily planning. Let's explore how this powerful tool can help you streamline your schedule and optimize your time management.

Calendar Integration

Integrating ChatGPT with your calendar applications, such as Google Calendar or Microsoft Outlook, allows you to manage your appointments and reminders effortlessly. To set this up, you would start by linking ChatGPT to your calendar app through API connections, often provided within the app's settings under 'Integrations.' Once connected, you can directly communicate with ChatGPT to add, remove, or update events. For instance, you might say, "Add a team meeting for next Thursday at 3 PM to my calendar," ChatGPT will handle the rest, creating the event and even sending invites to participants if required. This integration saves you the hassle of manually entering each appointment and ensures that your calendar is always up-to-date with real-time adjustments.

Furthermore, you can set up ChatGPT to send you daily schedule briefings. Each morning, you could receive a concise overview of your appointments and important daily reminders directly from ChatGPT. This proactive approach means you never miss an important meeting or deadline, as ChatGPT keeps you informed and prepared for the day's commitments.

Scheduling Meetings

Coordinating meetings, especially with multiple participants, can often be tedious, involving back-and-forth communication to finalize timings. ChatGPT simplifies this process by interacting with the calendars of all involved parties. If you need to schedule a meeting, simply instruct ChatGPT with your availability and the email addresses of the participants, such as, "Schedule a 30-minute marketing discussion sometime next Wednesday afternoon with [email address] and [email address]" ChatGPT will analyze the calendars, find a slot that works for everyone, and set the meeting, all while keeping you updated. It can also handle rescheduling requests, ensuring that changes are communicated effectively to all participants.

Moreover, ChatGPT can automatically set reminders for these meetings. You can specify if you want a reminder a day before or just a few hours prior, and ChatGPT will ensure you're notified in advance, helping you manage your time efficiently.

Task Prioritization

Prioritizing tasks effectively is key to productive time management. ChatGPT can assist you by classifying tasks based on urgency and importance. You can list your tasks and ask ChatGPT to organize them into categories such as 'Urgent,' 'High Priority,' 'Medium Priority,' and 'Low Priority.' For example, after providing ChatGPT with a list of tasks such as emails to respond to, reports to complete, and meetings to prepare for, you might ask, "Which of these tasks should I prioritize for today?" ChatGPT will analyze the list and your upcoming deadlines to suggest a prioritized task list.

This prioritization helps you focus your efforts on what truly matters each day. It reduces the stress of handling too many things at once and increases your productivity by ensuring that critical tasks are completed on time.

Time Management Tips

Finally, ChatGPT can offer personalized time management advice to help you make the most of your day. Based on your typical schedule and workload, ChatGPT can suggest strategies such as time blocking, allocating specific blocks of time for different tasks, or the Pomodoro Technique, which involves working in short sprints with breaks in between to boost focus and stamina. Simply ask, "How can I manage my time better?" ChatGPT will provide tips tailored to your activities and preferences.

For instance, if you find your afternoons less productive, ChatGPT might suggest scheduling more demanding tasks in the morning when your energy levels are higher, reserving lighter tasks for later in the day. It can also remind you to take regular breaks to prevent burnout, ensuring you maintain a steady pace throughout the day without compromising your well-being.

By leveraging ChatGPT in these ways, you transform managing your personal schedules from a daunting task to a more controlled and enjoyable part of your daily routine. Whether through seamless calendar integration, efficient meeting coordination, strategic task prioritization, or personalized time management tips, ChatGPT provides the tools to enhance how you plan and execute your day, leaving you more time and energy to focus on achieving your goals and enjoying your life.

4.3 ChatGPT for Health and Wellness

In today's fast-paced world, maintaining an optimal level of health and wellness can sometimes feel like a juggling act. Fortunately, ChatGPT can serve as a dependable resource, guiding you through various aspects of health management, from fitness routines to mental well-being. Integrating AI into your health regimen ensures you receive personalized advice and support tailored to your lifestyle and needs.

Fitness Routine Suggestions

Creating a fitness routine that aligns with your goals, current fitness level, and available resources is essential for effective workouts. ChatGPT can help craft a customized workout plan if you're unsure where to start. Begin by sharing your fitness objectives, whether it's weight loss, muscle building, or enhancing cardiovascular health. Additionally, provide details about your current fitness level and any equipment you can access; this could range from a fully-equipped gym to a yoga mat and resistance bands at home or without equipment.

For example, if your goal is to improve general fitness and you have minimal equipment, you might ask ChatGPT, "Can you create a 30-minute home workout plan for beginners with no equipment?" Based on your inputs, ChatGPT could suggest a routine including bodyweight exercises such as push-ups, sit-ups, and air squats, combined with intervals of jumping jacks or running in place to raise your heart rate. Each exercise would come with suggested repetitions and sets, adjusted to ensure they provide a challenge without being overwhelming. This approach helps establish a feasible and effective fitness routine. It adapts as your fitness level progresses, offering more complex combinations or incorporating new exercises to keep the routine engaging and challenging.

Dietary Recommendations

Nutrition plays a critical role in achieving health and wellness goals. ChatGPT can provide dietary recommendations that consider your specific nutritional needs, food preferences, and any dietary restrictions you might have. Start by discussing your health objectives with ChatGPT, such as losing weight, gaining muscle, or managing a health condition like diabetes. Also, mention any dietary preferences or restrictions, such as veganism or gluten intolerance.

For instance, if you're aiming to increase protein intake as part of a muscle-building regimen and you follow a plant-based diet, you might ask, "What are high-protein vegetarian meals that are easy to prepare?" ChatGPT can then offer a variety of recipes and meal ideas, such as lentil soup, quinoa salads, or tofu stir-fries, each detailed with ingredient lists and simple preparation steps. This personalized guidance helps you make informed dietary choices that contribute to reaching your physical health goals and fit seamlessly into your dietary preferences, ensuring sustainability and enjoyment in your eating habits without wasting time filtering through search results on the internet.

Mental Health Check-ins

Taking care of your mental health is as important as maintaining physical health. ChatGPT can assist in daily mental health check-ins, providing a safe space to express feelings, reflect on stressors, or simply unload thoughts. These check-ins can be as simple as prompting ChatGPT with, "I'm feeling stressed about work today. What can I do?" ChatGPT might suggest several stress management techniques, such as deep breathing exercises, short meditative practices, or even engaging in a hobby to divert your mind and ease stress.

Moreover, ChatGPT can encourage mindfulness and help you cultivate a habit of reflecting on your day-to-day experiences. This regular practice of self-reflection aids in recognizing patterns in thoughts and emotions, potentially uncovering triggers for anxiety or stress and empowering you to manage them more effectively. Over time, these check-ins can improve emotional resilience and help you better understand your mental health needs.

Sleep Hygiene Advice

Good sleep hygiene is fundamental to overall health, impacting everything from physical recovery to mental clarity. If you struggle with sleep, ChatGPT can offer advice on establishing routines that promote restful sleep. You might ask, "How can I improve my bedtime routine to get better sleep?" ChatGPT could then suggest various techniques, such as establishing a consistent bedtime, creating a pre-sleep ritual involving activities like reading or taking a warm bath, and avoiding stimulants such as caffeine and electronic devices close to bedtime.

Additionally, ChatGPT can provide guidance on the ideal sleep environment, recommending conditions that enhance sleep quality, such as the optimal room temperature, the use of blackout curtains to minimize light, or the benefits of white noise machines. By implementing these suggestions, you can create a conducive sleep environment that not only helps you fall asleep more quickly but also achieve deep, uninterrupted sleep, ultimately enhancing your daily energy levels and overall health.

Through these personalized interactions, ChatGPT acts as a comprehensive health and wellness advisor, addressing various aspects of your well-being. Whether it's crafting tailored fitness routines, providing dietary guidance, supporting mental health, or fostering better sleep habits, ChatGPT ensures that you have the tools and knowledge to lead a healthier, more balanced life. As you continue to utilize these features, you'll find that maintaining health and wellness becomes more integrated and manageable, allowing you to enjoy the benefits of a well-rounded and healthy lifestyle.

4.4 Financial Planning and Budgeting with ChatGPT

Navigating the often complex world of personal finance can sometimes feel overwhelming, but with tools like ChatGPT, you can simplify and take control of your financial future. Whether creating a realistic budget, conducting regular financial health assessments, exploring investment strategies, or managing debt, ChatGPT can be invaluable in your journey to financial stability and growth.

Budget Creation and Management

Creating and managing a personal budget is crucial for financial well-being, but many find the process tedious or complicated. ChatGPT simplifies this by helping you construct a budget that aligns with your income, expenses, and financial goals. First, you would provide ChatGPT with details about your regular income sources and recurring expenses such as rent, utilities, groceries, and transportation. For example, you might say, "My monthly income is $3,000, and my fixed expenses total $1,500." With this information, ChatGPT can help categorize your spending into 'needs,' 'wants,' and 'savings,' suggesting allocations based on standard budgeting principles like the 50/30/20 rule—which allocates 50% of income to needs, 30% to wants, and 20% to savings. Additionally, ChatGPT can offer general financial rules of thumb, such as the 75/15/10 saving and investing guideline, to help you manage your finances more effectively.

Furthermore, ChatGPT can assist in setting up a system to track your expenses and monitor your budget adherence. This might involve linking ChatGPT to your financial accounts or setting up notifications for when you approach spending limits in certain categories. This proactive management ensures that you stay on track with your budget, making adjustments as needed to avoid overspending and meet your financial goals. For instance, if you consistently overspend on dining out, ChatGPT can alert you when you are near your monthly limit or suggest cheaper dining alternatives to help you stay within budget.

Financial Health Check-ups

Regular check-ups are as vital for your financial health as they are for your physical health. ChatGPT can conduct these assessments by reviewing your financial data and evaluating your spending habits, savings, debt levels, and overall financial progress. You might ask, "How am I doing financially this quarter?" ChatGPT would analyze the data, compare your current spending against your budget, check how much you've saved versus your goals, and review debt reductions.

This review helps you understand where you stand financially, highlighting successes and identifying improvement areas. For instance, if your savings are on track but debt reduction is lagging, ChatGPT might suggest revising your budget to allocate more towards debt repayment. This regular appraisal keeps you informed and proactive about managing your finances, ensuring you always work towards greater financial health and stability.

Investment Ideas and Tips

Investing can be an effective way to grow your wealth, but understanding where and how to invest can be daunting. ChatGPT simplifies this process by providing general investment recommendations based on your financial situation and risk tolerance. After discussing your investment goals and how much risk you are comfortable taking, ChatGPT can suggest a range of investment options. Whether you are interested in stocks, bonds, mutual funds, or real estate, ChatGPT can outline the potential benefits and risks associated with each option. ChatGPT can also provide basic asset allocations based on your financial circumstances and risk tolerance.

For example, ChatGPT might recommend looking into high-quality bonds or dividend-paying stocks if you are a conservative investor interested in steady returns. It can also guide you in diversifying your investments by allocating assets across asset classes specific to your goals, potentially mitigating risk and enhancing returns. Additionally, ChatGPT can provide information regarding market trends, historical data, and economic factors that might affect your investments, helping you make informed decisions on when to buy, hold, or sell your assets.

Debt Management Advice

Effective debt management is key to financial freedom, and ChatGPT can offer guidance on approaching and reducing your liabilities. By analyzing your debt levels, interest rates, and financial capacity, ChatGPT can develop a debt repayment plan tailored to your circumstances. This might include strategies like the debt snowball method, where you focus on paying off smaller debts first to build momentum, or the debt avalanche method, where you pay down debts with the highest interest rates first to minimize overall interest payments.

ChatGPT can also advise on negotiating with creditors for better repayment terms or consolidating multiple debts into a single loan with a lower interest rate. This personalized advice helps you tackle your debt effectively, reducing financial stress and paving the way for a debt-free future. Moreover, by regularly consulting ChatGPT, you can keep track of your progress and adjust your repayment strategies as needed, ensuring that you remain on the fastest and most efficient path to eliminating your debt.

4.5 ChatGPT as a Study Buddy

In Chapter Three, we explored how ChatGPT can enhance business productivity by aiding learning and research, particularly in a professional or academic context. While the previous section focused on learning within a business framework, this chapter highlights how ChatGPT can support personal educational goals. Here, we will discuss how ChatGPT can serve as a study buddy in your personal life, helping you with language practice, homework assistance, creating study plans and schedules, and suggesting educational resources. This personalized approach ensures that ChatGPT can assist you in a more relaxed and individualized setting, making your learning journey enjoyable and efficient.

Language Practice

Embracing a new language opens doors to a richer understanding of different cultures and enhances cognitive abilities. ChatGPT is an invaluable companion in this linguistic journey, offering a range of interactive practices catering to various learning stages, from beginners grappling with basics to advanced learners refining their fluency. To begin with, you might want to establish a foundation in vocabulary and basic sentence structures. Here, ChatGPT can act as an interactive flashcard system. You could input a list of words or phrases. ChatGPT could quiz you, provide definitions, or ask you to construct sentences using new words, reinforcing your memory and recall.

Transitioning from static vocabulary exercises to dynamic conversational practice, ChatGPT can simulate real-life interactions, allowing you to apply what you've learned in practical scenarios. For instance, if you're learning Spanish and planning a trip to Spain, you might practice ordering food or asking for directions. Phrases like, "How do I say, 'A table for two, please' in Spanish?" or "What's the Spanish word for 'train station'?" can be posed to ChatGPT. It responds with translation corrections and suggestions on pronunciation, usage, and cultural nuances that textbooks often miss. This learning method is more engaging and builds confidence in using the language in everyday situations, making the learning process both effective and enjoyable.

Homework Help

Tackling homework across various subjects can sometimes be daunting, especially when complex concepts and tough assignments pile up. ChatGPT is a resourceful tool for breaking these complex ideas into understandable segments. Suppose you're struggling with a physics problem about Newton's laws or need clarification on a historical event like the French Revolution. By inputting the specific question or topic into ChatGPT, you can receive detailed explanations, step-by-step problem-solving guidance, or historical summaries. For example, asking, "Can you explain Newton's third law with examples?" would prompt ChatGPT to provide the textbook definition and real-world applications, such as how rocket propulsion illustrates this law.

Furthermore, ChatGPT can assist in structuring essays or reports. Suppose you're assigned to write about climate change's impacts. In that case, ChatGPT can help outline key points, such as global warming, effects on ecosystems, and socio-economic implications, organizing your research into a coherent structure. This helps craft a well-rounded essay with a clear argument, ensuring your homework meets the academic criteria and engages the reader with well-presented information and insights.

Study Plans and Schedules

As exams approach, effective study planning becomes crucial. ChatGPT can aid in creating personalized study schedules that optimize your revision and prepare you thoroughly for exam day. You would start by telling ChatGPT the number of subjects, the days available for study, and any particular priorities or challenging areas. ChatGPT could then generate a study timetable that allocates time blocks for each subject, ensuring you cover all necessary material without cramming. It might suggest alternating between subjects or topics to keep your study sessions dynamic and mentally stimulating.

Additionally, ChatGPT can incorporate effective study techniques into your schedule. Techniques like spaced repetition for memorization or active recall sessions can be interspersed throughout your plan. This way, you follow a time structure and employ strategies that enhance learning retention, making your preparation more productive and less stressful.

Educational Resource Suggestions

While textbooks and classroom notes are invaluable, supplementing them with diverse educational resources can enhance your understanding and interest in a subject. ChatGPT can recommend a variety of resources tailored to your specific learning needs and interests. ChatGPT might suggest animated videos that visually explain complex reactions if you're a visual learner struggling with organic chemistry. Alternatively, if you prefer interactive learning, it could direct you to simulations or online quizzes that provide immediate feedback and explanations, helping you grasp difficult concepts through practice.

Moreover, ChatGPT can point you to academic journals, expert blogs, or educational podcasts for those seeking deeper insights or alternative explanations. For instance, if you're researching modernist literature, ChatGPT could recommend scholarly articles discussing the cultural contexts of works by T.S. Eliot and Virginia Woolf or podcasts where experts debate their narrative styles and themes. These resources broaden your perspective and enrich your academic experience, making learning a more engaging and comprehensive process. Through ChatGPT's guidance, you can access knowledge that complements traditional learning methods, fostering a more rounded and informed approach to your studies.

4.6 Entertainment and Leisure: ChatGPT as Your Guide

In entertainment and leisure, a versatile tool like ChatGPT can enrich your experiences by offering personalized suggestions and creative ideas that align with your interests and preferences. Whether you're a cinephile looking for your next favorite movie, an avid reader in search of a captivating book, an adventurer planning your next excursion, or a hobbyist seeking to expand your creative pursuits, ChatGPT is equipped to guide you through each of these aspects, enhancing the joy and fulfillment derived from your leisure activities.

Movie and Book Recommendations

Diving into a good book or movie offers relaxation and opens worlds of imagination and insight. ChatGPT can personalize recommendations based on your past likes and interests, ensuring that every suggestion resonates with your tastes. Suppose you enjoyed a movie like "Inception" and are looking for something similar, or you loved a book such as "1984" by George Orwell and want to explore similar genres. You could ask ChatGPT, "Can you recommend movies similar to 'Inception' or books like '1984'?" Using its extensive database and understanding of your preferences, ChatGPT would analyze elements common to your favorites—thematic depth, narrative style, or genre—and suggest a list of movies or books you will likely enjoy. This tailored approach saves you time searching and enhances your entertainment experience by consistently aligning with your unique preferences.

Travel Planning and Local Exploration

Planning travel to distant lands or local attractions can be an exciting yet daunting task. ChatGPT simplifies this process by helping you craft detailed itineraries based on your interests, the duration of your trip, and attendees. If you're planning a weekend getaway to a city like San Francisco, you might ask, "What are the must-visit places in San Francisco over a weekend?" ChatGPT could then outline a comprehensive itinerary that includes visiting the Golden Gate Bridge, exploring Fisherman's Wharf, and dining at renowned local eateries. Additionally, it can provide insights into local attractions that are less touristy but equally enriching, offering you a blend of popular and unique experiences.

Moreover, ChatGPT can assist in logistical planning by suggesting the best times to visit attractions, making reservations, or providing tips on local transportation. This thorough planning tool ensures your travels are enjoyable and maximally efficient, allowing you to explore and experience more within your available time.

Creative Hobbies

Fostering creative hobbies enriches your free time and promotes mental well-being and personal satisfaction. Whether you're interested in starting a new hobby like painting or enhancing an existing one like DIY home projects, ChatGPT can provide step-by-step guides, creative ideas, and practical tips. For instance, if you're new to watercolor painting, you might ask, "How do I start with watercolor painting, and what are some easy projects?" ChatGPT could offer basic techniques, suggest starter kits, and provide simple project ideas like painting a sunset or a floral composition. ChatGPT can suggest advanced projects or techniques for more seasoned hobbyists, such as creating a DIY home decor piece from recycled materials. This guidance helps you start and sustain hobbies and encourages continuous learning and creativity, making your leisure time more productive and enjoyable.

Game and Puzzle Creation

Playing games and puzzles can be a delightful way to challenge your mind and share fun moments with friends and family. ChatGPT can assist you in creating custom games and puzzles tailored to your group's interests and complexity preferences. Whether you want to design a trivia quiz about classic films, a crossword puzzle based on your favorite books, or a scavenger hunt for a family gathering, ChatGPT can provide the framework, rules, and content for these games. You might say, "I need a trivia game for a movie night with friends." ChatGPT would then generate questions, multiple-choice answers, and even scoring guidelines based on popular movies or specific genres you enjoy. This personalized approach makes game nights more engaging and ensures they are inclusive and enjoyable for all participants, fostering a spirit of community and shared joy.

In integrating ChatGPT into your entertainment and leisure activities, you gain a personalized guide that enhances your experiences, whether by recommending media that matches your tastes, simplifying travel planning, inspiring creative pursuits, or enriching your social gatherings with custom games. This chapter illustrates the practical applications of ChatGPT in enhancing leisure activities and encourages you to explore and embrace new experiences, enriching your life with enjoyment and creativity. As we conclude this exploration of ChatGPT's role in entertainment and leisure, we see how this AI tool serves practical needs and enhances life's joyful moments, making every leisure activity more engaging and personalized.

4.7 Interactive Task: Create a Meal Plan

Healthy meal planning is essential for maintaining a balanced diet and overall wellness. With ChatGPT's assistance, you can create personalized meal plans that cater to your specific dietary needs and preferences. This interactive task is designed to help beginners leverage ChatGPT to plan, review, and refine their meals, making healthy eating manageable and enjoyable. Following the steps outlined below, you'll learn how to use ChatGPT to develop a sustainable and nutritious meal routine.

First, ask ChatGPT to create a healthy meal plan for the week, remembering to use the perfect prompt formula where necessary. Once you receive the meal plan, review it to ensure it meets your dietary needs and preferences. If you have any dietary restrictions, such as lactose intolerance or gluten sensitivity, ask ChatGPT to adjust the meal plan accordingly. Next, based on the meal plan, use a prompt to compile a shopping list of the ingredients you'll need for the week. This will help streamline your grocery shopping and ensure you have all the necessary items. Finally, ask ChatGPT for recipes based on the meals provided and prepare for the upcoming week. You can use this as merely an exercise or follow the weekly meal plan.

At the end of the week, reflect on your experience. Note any feedback or adjustments you might need for the meal plan. Use ChatGPT to refine the plan further based on your feedback. Following these steps will give you a personalized and healthy meal plan that suits your dietary needs and preferences. This interactive task will help you develop a sustainable, healthy eating habit with the assistance of ChatGPT.

Conclusion

Congratulations on completing Chapter Four! You've explored how ChatGPT can enhance various aspects of your life, from managing daily routines and finances to supporting your educational goals and planning travel itineraries. By leveraging ChatGPT's capabilities, you've taken significant steps toward improving your well-being and productivity.

As we progress, we must consider the broader context of using AI daily. In the next chapter, we will move into a deeper analysis of the ethical use and social implications of ChatGPT. This section will guide you through the responsible and mindful use of AI technology, ensuring that your interactions with ChatGPT and similar tools are beneficial and aligned with ethical standards. Get ready to explore the critical considerations of integrating AI into our personal and professional lives, fostering a future where technology enhances our experiences while respecting societal values.

Ethical Use and Social Implications

Now that we have explored the foundations of AI and ChatGPT let's examine the ethical issues surrounding this technology. In a world increasingly driven by data, understanding the ethical implications of using powerful AI tools like ChatGPT is not just prudent—it's imperative. As you begin to integrate AI into your daily interactions, whether for work, learning, or personal growth, it becomes crucial to consider what AI can do and how it does it. The ethical use of AI, particularly regarding data privacy, is a cornerstone in fostering trust and safety in technology. This chapter will explore the nature of data exchange in AI systems, how this data is handled, and provide best practices to safeguard your information. By understanding these aspects, you can ensure your journey with AI remains secure and aligned with your values.

5.1 Understanding Data Privacy in ChatGPT Interactions

Data privacy concerns often arise when interacting with an AI like ChatGPT. Every query you input and every response you receive involves exchanging information that could be personal or sensitive. Understanding the nature of this data exchange is the first step towards using AI responsibly. When you ask ChatGPT for travel advice, for example, you might share details about your location, preferences, and timing—information that could potentially be misused if not appropriately handled.

AI systems like ChatGPT process and store vast amounts of data to learn and make informed responses. This data can include directly entered information as well as derived data generated from your interactions and choices. For instance, if you frequently ask about vegan recipes, the system might infer a dietary preference. AI's ability to aggregate and analyze data raises significant privacy concerns. The potential for data breaches or misuse is not just a theoretical risk; it impacts people's lives and choices.

Adopting best practices for data privacy is crucial to navigating these waters safely. One effective strategy is anonymizing your data. When interacting with ChatGPT, do not provide personally identifiable information unless absolutely necessary. For instance, you can ask for restaurant recommendations without disclosing your exact location—perhaps specify the city or town instead of your address. Additionally, familiarizing yourself with the privacy settings of the platform hosting the AI, such as OpenAI's ChatGPT, is essential. These settings often allow you to control what data is stored and how it's used.

Moreover, compliance with data protection regulations like the EU's General Data Protection Regulation (GDPR) is crucial for any platform handling personal data. GDPR and similar regulations in other jurisdictions aim to protect personal data and ensure users' privacy. They require that data be collected legally and under strict conditions and that those who collect and manage it are obliged to protect it from misuse and exploitation. As a user, understanding these protections helps you know your rights and the obligations of AI providers, making you a more informed and empowered technology user.

Navigating the ethical landscape of AI interactions necessitates a balanced approach that respects user privacy while leveraging the benefits of AI. By understanding the nature of data exchange, how AI systems handle this data, and the best practices for protecting your personal information, you can confidently engage with AI like ChatGPT, knowing you are taking the necessary steps to safeguard your privacy. As we continue to explore the ethical use of AI, remember that each interaction is an opportunity to ensure that technology works for us, enhancing our lives while upholding our values and rights.

5.2 Misinformation Risks and How to Mitigate Them

In the realm of AI-driven technologies like ChatGPT, misinformation can subtly seep into interactions, often due to the biases inherent in the training data or the limitations of the algorithms themselves. When AI systems are trained on skewed or incomplete data, they can inadvertently generate misleading or factually incorrect responses. This is particularly concerning in scenarios where decisions are made based on the information provided by AI, such as in financial advising, healthcare, or legal advice. Misinformation can arise not only from biased data but also from the way data is interpreted by the AI model. For instance, if an AI is trained predominantly on historical data that does not adequately represent current trends or minority reports, its outputs might not accurately reflect present realities.

Detecting misinformation in AI outputs is crucial and starts with developing a keen sense of critical evaluation. As a user, you should approach AI-generated content with a healthy skepticism, especially in subjects that are complex or have significant implications based on the accuracy of the information. Techniques to detect misinformation include cross-referencing AI responses with up-to-date and reliable sources and considering the consensus among experts in the subject matter. Additionally, paying attention to the language used by AI can also provide clues; overly simplistic explanations or responses that lack depth in technical discussions might indicate that the AI does not fully understand the topic, increasing the risk of inaccuracies.

Correcting misinformation is a multifaceted approach that involves both immediate and long-term strategies. In the short term, providing feedback to the

AI system when inaccuracies are detected helps refine its responses. Most AI platforms, including those powering ChatGPT, allow users to flag incorrect or misleading information, which can then be used to adjust the model's learning process. For a more long-term solution, retraining the AI model on a broader, more balanced, and continually updated dataset ensures that the information it generates is accurate and reflects the latest knowledge. This retraining process must be ongoing, as the accumulation of new data and the evolution of facts and societal norms never cease.

Promoting information literacy is fundamentally about empowering you and others to discern the quality and reliability of information better, whether it comes from AI or human sources. Understanding how to assess the credibility of sources, the importance of context when interpreting facts, and the common pitfalls in logical reasoning are all skills that enhance your ability to use AI like ChatGPT effectively and safely. Educational initiatives focusing on these skills are vital, particularly in schools, universities, and professional training. They ensure that as AI becomes more integrated into everyday life, users are equipped to use these tools and challenge and critique them constructively. By fostering a culture that values and understands the principles of information literacy, we ensure that society can enjoy the benefits of AI without falling prey to its potential pitfalls.

5.3 Human-in-the-Loop: Balancing AI and Human Oversight

The 'Human-in-the-Loop' (HITL) concept is pivotal in integrating AI systems like ChatGPT into sectors where decisions significantly impact human lives. Essentially, HITL refers to the active involvement of human operators in the functioning and decision-making processes of AI systems, ensuring that despite the autonomy of the technology, human judgment and oversight remain central. This approach is crucial for maintaining ethical standards and accountability and leveraging human expertise to guide and improve AI decision-making. The importance of HITL cannot be overstated, particularly in scenarios where

AI's autonomous operations could lead to significant consequences without human mediation.

Implementing human oversight in AI systems is observable in various industries and contexts. For example, in content moderation on social media platforms, AI algorithms are employed to filter and flag inappropriate content. However, human moderators play a critical role in reviewing these flags to make nuanced decisions that the AI might not be capable of due to limitations in understanding context and cultural nuances. Similarly, in healthcare, AI systems can analyze patient data and suggest diagnoses and treatments. Still, healthcare professionals must review these suggestions and make the final decisions, considering the AI's input as one of several critical resources. These examples highlight how human expertise and ethical reasoning are irreplaceable, ensuring that AI is a support tool rather than a replacement for human judgment.

The benefits of integrating human intuition with AI's capabilities are manifold. Firstly, it enhances the reliability of AI systems by incorporating human oversight to catch and correct errors that the AI might not recognize. This hybrid model can significantly reduce the risk of harm from unchecked AI decisions. Secondly, human-AI collaboration allows leveraging AI's ability to process and analyze large datasets quickly while benefiting from human creativity and ethical reasoning. This collaboration leads to more innovative solutions that neither humans nor AI could achieve alone. Moreover, involving humans in AI processes helps in training AI systems to become more accurate and aligned with human values, as continuous human feedback can guide the AI's learning process and adjustment.

However, integrating human oversight with AI systems is not without challenges. One major challenge is the scalability of human involvement. As AI systems become more complex and widely used, the demand for human oversight can strain resources and become a bottleneck in processes that are designed to be enhanced by AI. Additionally, there is the risk of human bias and error being introduced into AI systems. Humans are not infallible, and their judgments can be influenced by subjective factors or incorrect information, which can reinforce these biases in AI behaviors.

To address these challenges, developing structured protocols for human-AI interaction is essential. Establishing clear guidelines on the roles and responsibilities of humans in AI-driven processes can help maintain the balance between leveraging AI's capabilities and ensuring responsible oversight. Training programs for human operators should also emphasize ethical considerations and bias awareness to mitigate the risk of skewed human inputs. Moreover, employing diverse human supervisors can help offset individual biases, leading to more balanced and objective oversight.

Adopting a HITL approach where humans and AI collaborate effectively requires thoughtful design and continuous refinement of processes. It involves technical adjustments and a cultural shift towards recognizing the value of both human and artificial intelligence. By fostering an environment where AI is seen as a tool to augment human capabilities rather than replace them, we can leverage the strengths of both to achieve more ethical, reliable, and effective outcomes in AI applications.

5.4 The Future of Work with AI Assistants

As previously discussed, AI assistants like ChatGPT are increasingly becoming integral components of the modern workplace, reshaping industries and workflows profoundly. Integrating AI tools in sectors ranging from customer service to content creation is not just about streamlining processes—it's about enhancing capabilities and forging new opportunities. For instance, in customer service, AI assistants can handle routine inquiries instantly and around the clock, freeing human agents to tackle more complex and sensitive cases that require empathy and nuanced judgment. This not only improves efficiency but also elevates the quality of service, offering customers timely responses and personalized interaction.

In the creative industries, AI tools are used to draft preliminary content outlines, suggest edits, and even generate creative content ideas based on trend analysis. This capability allows content creators to focus more on refining their work and engaging with their audiences in meaningful ways rather than getting bogged down by the initial stages of content development. Similarly, in fields such as law and healthcare, AI assistants help manage and sift through large volumes of data to highlight the most relevant information, thus speeding up research and reporting processes. This role of AI in data management underscores its potential as a transformative tool across various sectors, enabling professionals to make more informed decisions faster and with greater accuracy.

However, integrating AI in the workplace has challenges, particularly concerning employment. There is a genuine concern that AI could lead to job displacement, as tasks traditionally performed by humans are increasingly automated. While it's true that some roles may become less necessary, history shows that technological advancements are also very capable of creating new job opportunities. For example, the rise of AI has led to increased demand for AI trainers, who teach AI systems how to perform specific tasks, and AI ethicists, who ensure these systems operate within ethical boundaries. Prompt engineering is also becoming increasingly relevant as efficiently retrieving data from AI systems becomes more important. Moreover, as AI takes over more routine and administrative tasks, it frees human workers to focus on higher-level functions like strategy and innovation, leading to more fulfilling roles and new career paths.

Certain skills become particularly valuable in an AI-enhanced workplace in this evolving landscape. For one, digital literacy—understanding how to interact with and manage AI tools—is becoming essential. As you navigate a workplace augmented by AI, effectively collaborating with AI for data analysis, content generation, or customer interactions will set you apart as a proficient and versatile professional. Another critical skill is emotional intelligence. As AI handles more cognitive tasks, human-centric skills such as empathy, persuasion, and personal service become more important. These skills ensure that the human touch remains a central part of industries even as they leverage AI for growth and efficiency.

Advocating for ethical job design in implementing AI tools is crucial to ensure that technology augments rather than replaces human workers. Ethical job design involves creating roles that leverage AI's capabilities to enhance human work, not eliminate it. This can mean designing jobs where AI and humans collaborate, using AI's analytical capabilities to provide insights that human workers use to make strategic decisions or personalize customer interactions. For instance, a marketing professional could use AI-generated insights to understand customer preferences and craft more effective campaigns, combining the precision of AI with the creativity and empathy of the human mind. This approach preserves and enriches jobs, making them more impactful.

As AI continues to permeate various aspects of work, embracing these changes with an informed and proactive attitude is vital. By understanding the dynamic capabilities of AI, advocating for its ethical integration, and continuously adapting your skills, you can not only navigate but thrive in an AI-enhanced workplace. This readiness to adapt and grow with AI technologies ensures that your professional journey remains vibrant and forward-looking, marked by continuous learning and innovation.

5.5 Societal Impacts of Widespread AI Adoption

As artificial intelligence becomes ubiquitous in daily life, its influence extends far beyond the realms of technology and industry, seeping into the very fabric of society. The adoption of AI on a large scale is poised to transform cultural norms and social behaviors, reshape economic landscapes, redefine governance, and magnify global inequalities. Understanding these shifts is crucial for navigating the new societal dynamics that AI brings.

The cultural and social changes brought about by widespread AI adoption are profound and far-reaching. As AI technologies become integrated into everyday activities, from personalized shopping recommendations to automated customer service, they subtly alter people's expectations and behaviors. For instance, the instant gratification provided by AI-driven services can lead to decreased patience and heightened expectations for speed and efficiency in all areas of life. Moreover, as virtual assistants and chatbots become more sophisticated, they could shift the way people communicate, potentially leading to a preference for digital interaction over human contact in certain contexts. This could have broader implications for social skills and interpersonal relationships. Additionally, AI's role in content creation—from music to news articles—raises questions about authenticity and creativity, possibly changing how value is perceived in art and media. As these technologies curate and create content that reinforces specific patterns and preferences, they might also homogenize culture, diluting regional and individual uniqueness.

Economically, AI's integration into various sectors has the potential to both invigorate and disrupt. On the positive side, AI can drive efficiency, reduce costs, and unlock new entrepreneurial opportunities and business models. For example, predictive analytics powered by AI can help businesses anticipate market trends, optimize operations, and personalize services, leading to better customer satisfaction and economic growth. However, these benefits are accompanied by challenges such as job displacement. As AI automates routine tasks, there is a risk that jobs in sectors like manufacturing, retail, and administrative support could be significantly reduced. While new jobs will undoubtedly be created in tech and AI design, there is a concern about the mismatch between the skills required for these new roles and the capabilities of the current workforce, potentially leading to economic inequality and social unrest.

In the realm of governance and public policy, AI introduces both opportunities and obstacles. Governments can utilize AI to enhance public services, improve urban planning, and strengthen security. However, the use of AI in public decision-making and surveillance raises critical issues regarding privacy, civil liberties, and accountability. The potential for AI to be used for mass surveillance is particularly troubling, as it could lead to overreach by authorities and erosion of privacy rights. Decisions made by AI algorithms, such as those determining eligibility for loans or social benefits, must be transparent and subject to scrutiny to ensure fairness and justice. This highlights the need for robust regulatory frameworks that govern AI use, ensuring it aligns with ethical standards and public values.

Finally, the global spread of AI technologies is likely to exacerbate existing inequalities, both within and between countries. While affluent nations and individuals may have the resources to harness AI's advantages, developing countries might lag behind, lacking access to the technology and the expertise to implement it effectively. This digital divide could deepen global disparities, influencing economic opportunities, healthcare quality, and educational outcomes across regions. Addressing this issue requires concerted efforts from global stakeholders, including governments, tech companies, and international organizations, to ensure that AI technologies are accessible and beneficial to all. Strategies might include investing in digital infrastructure, fostering international collaborations for technology transfer, and implementing policies that encourage innovation while ensuring equitable distribution of its benefits.

As AI continues to evolve and permeate various aspects of life, its societal impacts—ranging from cultural shifts to economic transformations and governance challenges—must be carefully managed. By fostering a deep understanding of these dynamics, society can better prepare for and navigate the changes that AI brings, ensuring that the technology enhances human life while respecting ethical standards and promoting inclusivity and fairness.

5.6 Creating an Ethical Framework for ChatGPT Usage

As the boundaries of AI capabilities continue to expand, the importance of an ethical framework in developing and deploying technologies like ChatGPT becomes evident. This framework serves as a cornerstone, ensuring that AI operates within bounds that are effective, morally sound, and socially responsible. The rationale for this framework stems from the potential of AI to influence a wide range of human activities and decisions. Without a structured set of ethical guidelines, deploying AI technologies could lead to outcomes misaligned with societal values and individual rights, such as privacy breaches or unfair decision-making processes.

At the core of an ethical framework for AI like ChatGPT are principles that ensure users' transparency, accountability, fairness, and empowerment. Transparency involves clear communication about how AI systems operate and make decisions. This is crucial for building trust and allowing users and regulators to understand and assess the technology. Accountability refers to establishing mechanisms where responsible parties can be answerable for AI systems' actions. This helps maintain a check on AI operations, ensuring they adhere to declared values and legal standards.

Fairness is another pillar that ensures that AI systems do not embed or propagate biases that could lead to discriminatory practices. This involves careful scrutiny of the data used to train AI models like ChatGPT, ensuring it is representative and free of biases that could skew AI behavior. Lastly, user empowerment is about designing AI systems that enhance users' abilities without manipulating or diminishing the quality of human decision-making. This includes giving users control over how they interact with AI and how their data is used, ensuring the technology augments human capabilities without undermining them.

Implementing these ethical principles in real-world AI applications involves several steps. Initially, organizations need to define clear ethical guidelines that align with their core values and the expectations of their stakeholders, including users, regulatory bodies, and the general public. These guidelines should be integrated into the entire lifecycle of AI development, from the design and training phases to deployment and beyond. For instance, during the development of ChatGPT, developers can incorporate transparency by ensuring the AI's decision-making processes are interpretable by humans. Similarly, accountability can be addressed by establishing a clear protocol for monitoring AI performance and reporting on its operations.

Equally important is the continuous evaluation and adaptation of the ethical framework. As AI technologies and societal norms evolve, so too must the frameworks governing AI use. This involves regular assessments of AI performance and its impacts on users and society. It also includes updating ethical guidelines to address new challenges and opportunities as technology advances. For example, as ChatGPT becomes capable of more complex interactions, its developers should regularly review whether its responses adhere to evolving norms of fairness and inclusivity, making necessary adjustments in its training data and algorithms.

Additionally, fostering a culture of ethical AI use within organizations and among AI developers and users can reinforce these frameworks. This can be achieved through training programs, ethical audits, and open dialogue about the ethical implications of AI. By ingraining ethics into the fabric of organizational processes and the mindset of individuals who develop and deploy AI, the technology can be steered to contribute positively to society.

By embedding these ethical principles and practices into the development and use of AI, like ChatGPT, organizations can navigate the complex landscape where technology meets human values. This helps mitigate risks, fosters trust, and enhances the overall effectiveness and acceptance of AI technologies in society. As we move forward, the continuous refinement and application of these ethical guidelines will play a crucial role in shaping the future of AI, ensuring that it serves as a force for good, enhancing our capabilities and enriching our lives.

In summary, creating an ethical framework for AI usage, particularly for technologies like ChatGPT, is a technical necessity and a moral imperative. As we conclude this chapter, we recognize the importance of grounding AI advancements in strong ethical practices that uphold transparency, accountability, fairness, and user empowerment. This approach ensures that as AI technologies become more embedded in our daily lives and across various sectors, they do so in beneficial ways and aligned with broader societal values. Moving forward into the next chapter, we will explore specific case studies that highlight the practical applications and challenges of implementing AI in diverse contexts, providing deeper insights into the real-world implications of AI technologies.

5.7 Interactive Task

Reflect on how you currently use (or plan to use) AI tools like ChatGPT in your personal and professional life, identifying areas where ethical considerations might be relevant, such as data privacy, transparency, and potential biases in AI responses. List your ethical concerns, such as data privacy issues in customer service responses or potential biases in generated content. Using resources from this chapter and additional research, identify best practices for addressing these concerns, focusing on guidelines for data privacy, AI transparency, and bias mitigation. Finally, create a plan outlining steps to ensure your AI use is ethical, including implementing data privacy measures, ensuring transparency by communicating AI involvement to users, and regularly reviewing AI prompts to minimize bias. This plan will help you navigate and improve the ethical implications of using AI tools in daily interactions.

Now that we have explored the foundations of AI and ChatGPT, examining the ethical issues surrounding this technology is essential. In a world increasingly driven by data, understanding the ethical implications of using powerful AI tools like ChatGPT is not just prudent—it's imperative. As you integrate AI into your daily interactions, whether for work, learning, or personal growth, it becomes crucial to consider what AI can do and how it does it. The ethical use of AI, particularly regarding data privacy, is a cornerstone in fostering trust and safety in technology. This chapter delves into the nature of data exchange in AI systems, how this data is handled, and provides best practices to safeguard your information, ensuring your journey with AI remains secure and aligned with your values.

As we move forward, we will explore ChatGPT's advanced features and customization options. This next chapter will equip you with the knowledge to tailor AI interactions to suit your unique needs and preferences, enhancing the overall user experience. Get ready to unlock ChatGPT's full potential with advanced techniques and customization strategies.

Advanced Features and Customization

Welcome to Chapter Six! Now that you have a strong foundation in using ChatGPT and understand the ethical considerations, it's time to explore the advanced features and customization options that can further enhance your experience. Imagine discovering a secret passage in a familiar room that leads to new corridors and hidden treasures. That's akin to exploring the latest features and functionalities that updates to ChatGPT bring to users like you. Each update enhances the tool's existing capabilities and unveils fresh possibilities that can transform your interaction with this powerful AI. Many of these advanced features may require more technical skills or the help of the tech department of your organization, but the information is provided here for beginners so you can grow with the technology. This section examines the most recent upgrades to ChatGPT, helping you understand their significance and how you can leverage them to enrich both personal and professional aspects of your life.

6.1 Exploring the Latest Features in ChatGPT Updates

Overview of Updates

The landscape of technology, especially AI is continually evolving, and staying abreast of these changes ensures that you are maximizing the potential of tools like ChatGPT. Updates to ChatGPT have introduced a suite of enhancements designed to make the AI more intuitive, responsive, and versatile. For instance, newer versions have improved the model's understanding of nuanced language and context, making interactions more fluid and natural. There's also been a significant reduction in response times, so you can now have quicker interactions that feel more like conversing with a human. Additionally, updates have expanded the range of topics ChatGPT can discuss and provide advice on, from more in-depth business insights to complex scientific concepts, broadening the scope of its applicability.

Understanding Feature Enhancements

Each feature introduced in the latest updates is not just a technical upgrade but a gateway to enhanced user experience. For example, the enhanced understanding of context allows you to have extended conversations where ChatGPT remembers the thread of the discussion, a feature that mimics human-like memory in conversations. This means you can now discuss projects or plans across several interactions without repeating or summarizing previous messages. Imagine planning an event or discussing a business strategy over several days; ChatGPT's ability to recall previous interactions can add coherence and depth to the planning process, making it a more robust tool for project management and execution.

Moreover, improving response speed and understanding user intents significantly boost productivity. For professionals and students, this means less time waiting for responses and more time acting on the information provided.

Whether drafting emails, preparing for a presentation, or learning a new topic, these enhancements ensure that ChatGPT aligns more closely with your pace and demands, effectively becoming a more integrated part of your daily tools. These feature enhancements depend on the version selected when prompting ChatGPT.

Staying Informed on Updates

Keeping up-to-date with these developments is key to making the most of ChatGPT. One effective strategy is to subscribe to newsletters from AI and technology news sources that provide updates on ChatGPT and similar AI tools. These newsletters often cover the latest changes, provide insights into how the updates function, and sometimes offer tips on how to use new features effectively. Additionally, participating in online forums and communities focused on AI technology can be invaluable. Platforms like Reddit, Stack Exchange, or specialized LinkedIn groups allow you to engage with other users and experts who share insights and practical advice on navigating the updates, thus helping you understand and utilize the advanced features of ChatGPT more adeptly.

Leveraging Updates for Enhanced Performance

To fully benefit from the latest updates, it's crucial to incorporate these enhancements into your daily use of ChatGPT actively. Experiment with the new features in various contexts to see how they can best serve your needs. For instance, if you're a researcher, test the improved contextual understanding by having ongoing discussions on your research topic. Business professionals should try faster processing speeds for real-time decision-making during meetings or brainstorming sessions. By integrating these updated features into regular use, you can transform how you interact with ChatGTP—turning it from a simple conversational tool to an indispensable assistant that augments your capabilities and streamlines your tasks.

Through these updates, ChatGPT becomes more aligned with your personal and professional needs and continues redefining the boundaries of what AI can achieve in everyday applications. As you explore and adapt to these enhancements, you unlock new levels of productivity and engagement, ensuring your ChatGPT experience remains cutting-edge and deeply rewarding.

6.2 Fine-Tuning ChatGPT for Specific Industries

In an era where artificial intelligence molds the backbone of industry-specific solutions, tailoring ChatGPT to meet the healthcare, legal, and finance sectors' unique needs enhances its functionality and ensures its applications are precise and beneficial. Customizing ChatGPT involves adapting its responses to reflect the terminology, ethical considerations, and regulatory demands of specific fields, enhancing its utility as a professional tool. For instance, ChatGPT can be fine-tuned in healthcare to provide support in medical terminology management or to assist with patient data privacy, adhering to HIPAA regulations. Similarly, in the legal sector, it can be trained to understand and generate information pertinent to legal precedents or case law, while in finance, its customization might focus on compliance with financial regulations or analysis of market trends.

The process of fine-tuning ChatGPT for these industries begins with training the model on domain-specific datasets. This could involve feeding ChatGPT thousands of medical journals to prepare for deployment in healthcare settings or exposing it to vast financial reports and compliance documentation for finance applications. This training equips ChatGPT with the knowledge base and contextual understanding necessary to operate effectively within these sectors, making its interactions more relevant and insights more actionable.

It is important to note that fine-tuning and training the model for specific industries is not typically the end user's responsibility but is managed by organizations like OpenAI. OpenAI continuously updates and improves the model, ensuring it remains cutting-edge and applicable across various industries.

Additionally, several third-party companies integrate GPT models into industry-specific tools, making these tailored solutions readily available. For example, GPT-powered tools are designed explicitly for legal research, financial analysis, or medical record-keeping. Users interested in leveraging these advanced capabilities can search for and adopt these specialized tools, benefiting from the extensive work already done to adapt ChatGPT to their professional needs. This approach allows users to enjoy the advantages of AI without needing to undertake the complex process of training and fine-tuning models themselves.

Case Studies and Use Cases

A recent survey by Forbes Advisor (Image 6.1) highlights that businesses intend to use ChatGPT for various applications, including general responses, summarizing information, improving decision-making, translations, content creation, coding, and web design. These diverse use cases demonstrate the extensive potential of ChatGPT across different professional settings. Understanding these examples can help beginners identify how ChatGPT might best serve their specific needs.

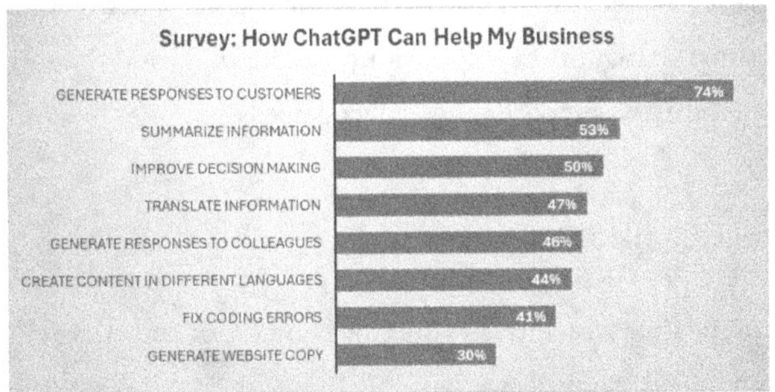

Image 6.1: Use Cases Survey

One illustrative case study is the integration of ChatGPT in a major hospital, where it was used to triage patient inquiries online before they reached human staff. The hospital reduced waiting times by customizing ChatGPT with medical knowledge and patient interaction protocols and significantly improved patient satisfaction. However, the challenge lies in continuously updating the

AI with the latest medical research and health protocols to maintain reliability. Another case involves a law firm that utilized ChatGPT to draft and review legal documents. The AI was trained on a comprehensive database of legal texts and was subsequently able to generate first drafts of contracts and legal briefs, fine-tuned by human lawyers. This sped up the drafting process and reduced the incidence of human error, though it required rigorous training to align with legal standards and practices.

In the tech industry, ChatGPT has streamlined customer support by providing instant, accurate responses to common technical issues. This improves customer satisfaction and frees up human agents to handle more complex queries. In marketing agencies, ChatGPT assists in generating creative content and conducting market analysis, helping teams stay ahead of trends and produce high-quality work efficiently.

These examples demonstrate how ChatGPT can be integrated into different sectors to enhance productivity and efficiency. For beginners, exploring these case studies can offer valuable insights into the varied applications of ChatGPT. You can leverage ChatGPT to drive innovation and achieve your goals by tailoring its uses to meet unique business requirements. Whether in healthcare, law, tech, or marketing, the key is continuously adapting and refining AI usage to align with industry standards and evolving needs.

Compliance Considerations

Ensuring compliance with industry-specific regulations and ethical standards is paramount when customizing ChatGPT. In healthcare, this involves aligning the AI's operations with patient confidentiality laws and medical ethics. In finance, it means ensuring that all financial advice or analysis provided by ChatGPT adheres to legal standards and market regulations. Moreover, transparency in how the AI operates, especially in how it processes and uses data, is crucial to maintaining trust and accountability. Establishing clear guidelines on data usage and integrating safeguards to protect sensitive information are essential steps in deploying a customized ChatGPT in any regulated industry.

By adhering to these principles and approaches, ChatGPT can be effectively customized to meet the specialized needs of various industries, enhancing its applicability and ensuring that its integration is both beneficial and compliant with professional standards. As industries continue to evolve and new challenges emerge, fine-tuning AI solutions like ChatGPT will be crucial in ensuring that these tools keep pace with changes and drive innovation and efficiency in professional practices.

6.3 Integrating ChatGPT with Other Software and Tools

Integrating ChatGPT with other software and tools through Application Programming Interfaces (APIs) opens up a world of possibilities, transforming how you interact with and utilize this powerful AI tool across various platforms. APIs act like bridges that allow different software systems to communicate and work together. For instance, integrating ChatGPT with your favorite project management tool or customer relationship management (CRM) system can enhance functionality and streamline operations. Let's start by breaking down the basics of API integration with ChatGPT. Essentially, APIs provide a set of rules and protocols for how software components should interact. When you integrate ChatGPT with another software via an API, you enable a direct line of communication between the two. This could mean having ChatGPT automatically pull data from another application to inform its responses or push its outputs to another system to trigger specific actions. This kind of integration is facilitated through API keys, essentially unique identifiers that authenticate a real-time data exchange between your ChatGPT instance and other software applications.

One practical application of API integration is enhancing CRM systems with ChatGPT. CRM systems are vital for managing a company's interactions with current and potential customers. By integrating ChatGPT, you can automate and personalize these interactions at scale. For example, when a customer sends a query through the CRM system, ChatGPT can instantly generate a personalized response based on the customer's previous interactions and preferences logged in the CRM. This speeds up response times and ensures that the communication is contextually relevant, significantly enhancing customer satisfaction. Moreover, ChatGPT can analyze customer feedback and interactions to identify trends and sentiments, providing valuable insights that can help refine marketing strategies and improve customer service practices. Currently, many CRMs offer AI enhancements, and this trend is expected to increase as the technology evolves.

Moving into the realm of project management, embedding ChatGPT into project management tools can revolutionize how projects are tracked and managed. Project management involves many tasks, from updating work progress to managing team communications. ChatGPT can automate routine updates and notifications, ensuring team members are always informed about project changes and deadlines without manual input. For instance, you could set up ChatGPT to send daily project status updates to all team members or use it to automatically assign tasks to team members based on their workload and expertise. This not only saves time but also helps maintain a high level of accuracy and efficiency in project communications. Several project management platforms integrate AI tools, and this integration is expected to improve and increase as the technology advances.

Encouraging creativity in integrating ChatGPT with unconventional tools can lead to innovative solutions that address unique challenges or enhance user experiences in unexpected ways. For example, integrating ChatGPT with virtual reality (VR) platforms could create immersive educational or training programs where ChatGPT, or similar AI technologies, provides real-time information or guidance to users navigating a virtual environment. Another innovative integration could be using AI with Internet of Things (IoT) devices. Picture a smart home where ChatGPT controls various devices based on conversational commands from the user, adjusting lighting and temperature or even suggesting recipes based on what's in your smart fridge. These examples highlight how flexible and adaptable ChatGPT can be when creatively integrated with different technologies, opening up a landscape of possibilities that can transform mundane tasks into interactive and engaging experiences.

Understanding ChatGPT's integrations with other software and tools provides a thorough foundation for leveraging its capabilities to enhance productivity and efficiency. This knowledge allows for creating more intuitive and responsive systems that better meet users' needs in various contexts. Whether it's through streamlining customer interactions, managing projects more effectively, or innovating with new tech combinations, the potential for ChatGPT to add value across different platforms and industries is immense, limited only by the creativity and vision of those who deploy it.

6.4 Building Custom Chatbots Using ChatGPT

Building a custom chatbot using ChatGPT can be an exciting journey, especially for beginners. This introduction aims to help you understand the full capabilities of ChatGPT as you grow your skills. Creating a chatbot that feels intelligent and intuitive isn't just about technical know-how—it's about understanding and anticipating the needs and reactions of its users. Starting with ChatGPT, you can design a chatbot that not only responds efficiently but also engages users in a meaningful way.

To get started, the first step is to clearly define your chatbot's purpose. This involves understanding what you need the chatbot to do. Is it to provide customer support, assist with e-commerce transactions, or offer information about a specific topic or service? Identifying the core purpose will guide every other aspect of the chatbot's development, from the dialogues it will handle to the personality it will project.

Next, you can begin by writing simple dialogue flows. Think of it as writing a script for how typical interactions should unfold. Start with common queries that users might ask, then outline logical and helpful responses from the chatbot. For example, if your chatbot is for customer support, consider the most common questions customers ask and write out how the chatbot should respond.

As you become more comfortable, you can start to consider the personality and tone of your chatbot. For instance, if your chatbot serves a professional consultancy, its language style should be formal and informative. Conversely, a chatbot for a youth-focused brand might have a more casual tone and playful personality.

Deploying your custom chatbot can start with simple steps, such as using it on a small scale within a website or social media platform. For example, you can use pre-built tools and plugins that integrate ChatGPT with platforms like Facebook Messenger or Slack, allowing you to see how the chatbot performs in real-world interactions.

Monitoring and refining your chatbot's performance is a crucial part of the process. Use feedback from users to make improvements. This can involve adjusting responses to better meet user needs or adding new functionalities based on what users are asking for.

Through these initial steps, building a chatbot with ChatGPT can be an exciting and rewarding project. You can create a functional tool that enhances user engagement and satisfaction by clearly defining its purpose, designing simple dialogues, personalizing its interactions, and deploying it in practical settings. As you dive into this process, remember that each choice and adjustment is a step towards creating a more connected and responsive experience for your users, leveraging the advanced capabilities of AI to meet and exceed the expectations of the digital age.

Remember, this is an introduction to help you understand ChatGPT's full capabilities. As you become more comfortable with the basics, you can explore more advanced customization options, potentially with the help of more technical resources or your organization's tech team.

6.5 Data Analysis with ChatGPT

Imagine having a tool that not only converses with you but also dives deep into oceans of data to fetch insights crucial for your business and research needs. ChatGPT, with its advanced data analysis capabilities, acts much like a seasoned data analyst capable of sifting through large datasets to extract meaningful information. This process involves parsing data, recognizing patterns, and drawing conclusions that can significantly influence decision-making processes.

Understanding Basic Data Analysis

To begin with data analysis, it is essential to understand the crucial role that high-quality data plays. Accurate and comprehensive data is the foundation of any meaningful analysis. Collecting, cleaning, analyzing, and interpreting data are fundamental to driving valuable insights. While ChatGPT cannot directly interact with datasets, it can guide you through each step by providing explanations, best practices, and examples, making the process more accessible to beginners. For instance, you can start by asking ChatGPT questions like, "How do I clean a dataset?" or "What are the common methods for data visualization?" ChatGPT can offer step-by-step instructions and explanations to help you understand these fundamental concepts and perform basic analyses, adding value to your data-driven decision-making process and enhancing the quality of your insights.

Leveraging ChatGPT for Data Cleaning

Data cleaning is crucial to data analysis to ensure accuracy and usability. ChatGPT can help you identify and correct errors in your dataset, such as missing values or outliers. Data ambiguity, such as inconsistent or unclear data entries, can pose significant challenges. For example, you might ask, "How do I handle missing data?" and receive guidance on techniques like imputation or removal of incomplete records, enhancing your data's reliability. Similarly, ChatGPT can suggest methods to standardize and clarify entries for ambiguous data, ensuring that your dataset is coherent and meaningful for analysis.

Analysis & Interpretation

Once your data is clean, ChatGPT can guide you through various analysis techniques. You can ask questions like, "How do I perform a regression analysis?" or "What are the steps to create a pivot table?" ChatGPT can provide explanations and examples, helping you apply these techniques to your dataset. This support makes learning and applying analytical methods more manageable. Interpreting the results of your data analysis is critical for making informed decisions. ChatGPT can also help you understand your findings and how to draw conclusions from your data. For example, you might ask, "What does a positive correlation between two variables indicate?" and receive a clear explanation that helps you understand the relationship between the variables.

Data Visualization

Data visualization is key to understanding and communicating your findings. ChatGPT can suggest different types of visualizations based on your data and the insights you want to convey. For instance, you might ask, "What type of chart should I use to compare monthly sales?" and ChatGPT can recommend bar charts, line graphs, or other visualizations. Additionally, if you're dealing with geographical data, you could ask, "How can I visualize regional sales performance?" ChatGPT might suggest using a heat map or a choropleth map. You can also inquire about the tools available to further enhance your data analysis toolkit. This helps you present your data clearly and effectively, making it easier to identify trends and patterns. Moreover, effective data visualization enhances your ability to share insights with stakeholders, facilitating better decision-making and strategic planning.

Many data visualization tools now offer AI-based assistance and guidance integrated by the provider. For example, tools like Tableau and Microsoft Power BI come with built-in AI capabilities that can help you create more insightful and interactive visualizations. These tools can automatically suggest the best charts based on your data, identify trends, and even provide predictive analytics. By integrating ChatGPT prompts with these advanced tools, you can generate summaries and insights that are then visually represented, making data insights more actionable and easier to interpret. This combination of AI-driven analysis and powerful visualization tools ensures that your data tells a story and drives informed decisions and strategic planning.

Predictive Analytics

The potential of using ChatGPT for predictive analytics is particularly exciting, as it opens up possibilities for forecasting future trends and behaviors. By training models with historical data, you can set up predictive analyses to forecast outcomes based on identified patterns. For example, historical sales data combined with promotional strategies can be analyzed in retail to forecast future sales trends. While ChatGPT cannot directly perform predictive analytics, it can guide you through the process and help interpret results. Even if you don't have deep expertise in predictive model building, ChatGPT can assist you in using tools like Python and Google Colab to create predictive models with a little hard work.

By starting with basic data analysis tasks and gradually exploring more advanced techniques, you can leverage ChatGPT as a powerful learning tool. This approach helps you build a strong foundation in data analysis and opens up new opportunities for insights and decision-making. As you continue to develop your skills, you'll find that data analysis becomes more accessible and rewarding, enhancing your ability to work with data effectively.

Practical Applications and Real-World Examples

In real-world scenarios, the applications of ChatGPT in data analysis are vast and impactful, spanning various industries and functions. Let's explore a few key areas where ChatGPT can significantly enhance data analysis capabilities, even for beginners.

Financial Sector

ChatGPT can assist in performing sentiment analysis on financial news articles, social media feeds, and market reports in the financial sector. For example, you might ask, "Considering this report, what is the sentiment around the company's outlook?" ChatGPT can help you analyze the tone and content of the report, providing a summary highlighting prevailing sentiment. By understanding these trends, investors can make more informed decisions about buying or selling stocks. Additionally, ChatGPT can guide you in building simple predictive models using historical stock data, enabling you to forecast stock price movements and market trends.

Healthcare

Data analysis can lead to better patient outcomes and more efficient healthcare delivery. ChatGPT can assist healthcare professionals by analyzing patient data to identify correlations between treatment plans and health outcomes. For example, "What are the common factors among patients who responded well to a specific treatment?" ChatGPT can help uncover patterns that might inform better clinical decisions by guiding you through data preprocessing and analysis. Furthermore, ChatGPT can provide insights into recent medical research, assisting practitioners to stay updated with the latest advancements and integrate them into their practice.

Marketing and Customer Insights

Understanding consumer behavior is crucial for marketers. ChatGPT can help analyze customer feedback, reviews, and social media interactions to identify common themes and sentiment trends. For instance, you could ask, "Based on these reviews, what are customers' main concerns about our product?" Chat-GPT can help categorize and summarize this feedback, providing actionable insights that inform product improvements and marketing strategies. Additionally, using historical sales data, ChatGPT can guide you in forecasting future sales trends and planning marketing campaigns accordingly.

Education

ChatGPT can assist in analyzing student performance data to identify areas where students may need additional support. For example, "Which topics do students struggle with the most in math?" ChatGPT can help you analyze aggregate data to pinpoint specific challenges and suggest targeted interventions. This data-driven approach ensures that educational resources are allocated effectively, enhancing student learning outcomes.

Environmental Science

Environmental scientists can leverage ChatGPT to analyze large datasets related to climate change, pollution levels, and biodiversity. For instance, "What trends can be observed in temperature changes over the past decade?" ChatGPT can guide you through visualizing and interpreting this data, helping to identify significant patterns and potential environmental impacts. By making complex data more accessible, ChatGPT supports informed decision-making in environmental conservation and policy development.

Business Operations

Businesses can use ChatGPT to streamline operations by analyzing operational data such as inventory levels, supply chain efficiency, and employee performance metrics. For example, "How can we optimize our inventory management?" ChatGPT can help analyze past sales data and inventory turnover rates, providing recommendations for inventory optimization. This leads to cost savings and improved efficiency in business operations.

By leveraging ChatGPT's guidance, even beginners can use advanced techniques to derive meaningful insights from their data. Whether in finance, healthcare, marketing, education, environmental science, or business operations, ChatGPT can enhance your data analysis capabilities and support data-driven decision-making. Starting with basic data analysis tasks and gradually exploring more advanced techniques allows you to build a strong foundation in data analysis. This approach enhances your ability to work with data effectively and opens up new opportunities for insights and decision-making. As you continue to develop your skills, data analysis becomes more accessible and rewarding, ultimately improving your proficiency and confidence in working with data. This increased understanding makes you more valuable in your current or future roles, equipping you with sought-after skills crucial in today's data-driven world.

6.6 Interactive Task

For this chapter's task, consider how ChatGPT can be integrated into your personal and professional life. Reflect on the various ways ChatGPT can be utilized, thinking about tasks that could be streamlined or enhanced. Identify one specific use case for ChatGPT in your professional life and one in your personal life. You can use ChatGPT to guide your brainstorming process if needed; also an excellent way to continue using the technology. As you identify these specific use cases, formulate prompts using the perfect prompt formula to ensure clarity and effectiveness in your interactions with ChatGPT. This exercise will help you integrate ChatGPT into your daily routine, making professional and personal tasks more manageable and efficient. Additionally, consider documenting your experience and the outcomes, as this can provide valuable insights and further refine your approach to leveraging ChatGPT in your life.

Now that you've explored the advanced features and customization options of ChatGPT, it's time to think about how to stay up-to-date with this rapidly evolving technological landscape. The final chapter, "Staying Ahead with Chat-GPT," will guide you on how to keep up with the latest advancements, updates, and best practices to ensure you continue to make the most of this powerful tool. Embracing the constant evolution of AI technology will enhance your personal and professional capabilities and prepare you to adapt and thrive in a future where AI plays an increasingly integral role.

Staying Ahead with ChatGPT

Welcome to Chapter Seven! As you've navigated through the advanced features and customization options of ChatGPT, you've unlocked powerful new capabilities and insights. But the journey doesn't stop here. In the fast-paced world of AI, staying current with technological advancements is crucial to maintaining your edge. This final chapter will empower you with strategies to keep up with the latest updates, trends, and best practices. By embracing the continuous evolution of ChatGPT and AI technologies in general, you will enhance your skills and ensure you are well-prepared to harness the full potential of AI in your personal and professional endeavors. Let's dive into how you can stay ahead and thrive in this ever-changing landscape.

7.1 Resources for Ongoing ChatGPT Education

Curated Online Courses and Tutorials

In the world of AI, education is key, and thankfully, it's also readily accessible. Online platforms like Coursera and Udacity offer structured courses specifically about AI and machine learning. These courses are crafted by experts from leading universities and innovative tech companies to deliver comprehensive learning experiences. For instance, Coursera's "AI For Everyone" by Andrew Ng provides a broad introduction to AI, covering the basics of algorithms, data needs, and ethical issues. For those specifically interested in ChatGPT, Udacity offers specialized programs that dive deep into natural language processing, teaching you how to build conversational AI models from scratch. These platforms typically provide a mix of video tutorials, readings, and hands-on projects, ideal for understanding the practical applications of concepts discussed.

Books and Academic Papers

While online courses offer structured learning paths, books and academic papers provide the depth and rigor necessary for a deeper understanding of AI. "Artificial Intelligence: A Guide for Thinking Humans" by Melanie Mitchell offers an insightful exploration of AI's capabilities and limitations, providing a solid foundation for beginners. For those looking to get into the specifics of conversational AI, reading seminal papers like "Attention Is All You Need" by Vaswani et al., which introduced the transformer model—the backbone of ChatGPT—is invaluable. These resources are typically peer-reviewed, ensuring high-quality and reliable information that covers both theoretical and practical aspects of AI. A quick search at Google Scholar will provide recent scholarly articles as academia continues to publish on the topic.

Interactive Learning Platforms

To truly master ChatGPT, one must move beyond passive learning and engage with interactive platforms that offer real-time feedback and practical experience. Codecademy, for example, offers an interactive course where you can learn by directly working with AI models. These platforms enhance your learning by allowing you to apply concepts in a controlled environment, experiment with code, and see the immediate impact of your adjustments. This hands-on approach is crucial for understanding the nuances of AI programming and model training.

Certification Programs

Numerous certification programs are available for those looking to validate their skills with a formal credential. These programs, offered by institutions like Microsoft and IBM, assess your AI and machine learning knowledge, culminating in a certification that can bolster your professional profile. They often cover a range of topics, from the basics of AI to more advanced subjects like neural networks and language models such as ChatGPT. Preparing for and obtaining these certifications can significantly sharpen your skills and understanding of AI technologies.

By engaging with these diverse learning resources, you equip yourself with the knowledge and skills needed to navigate the rapidly evolving field of AI. Whether through structured online courses, in-depth reading materials, interactive platforms, or professional certifications, each resource plays a crucial role in shaping your ability to leverage and innovate with AI tools like ChatGPT. As you continue to explore these educational opportunities, you'll find yourself not just keeping pace with AI advancements but actively contributing to them, ready to meet future challenges with expertise and confidence.

7.2 Joining Communities: Forums and Social Media Groups

Navigating the vast landscape of AI and ChatGPT can sometimes feel like exploring a new city without a map. However, joining dedicated communities on platforms such as Reddit, LinkedIn, and Discord can provide you with the guidance, companionship, and resources that make this journey easier and more enriching. These platforms host a variety of forums and groups where enthusiasts, experts, and beginners converge to discuss, share, and collaborate on topics related to AI and ChatGPT.

Finding the right community starts with identifying your interests and needs. On Reddit, for example, subreddits like r/MachineLearning, r/Artificial, and r/LanguageTechnology offer spaces where discussions range from technical advice and latest research to project showcases and troubleshooting tips. Each subreddit has its own culture and rules, so it's beneficial to spend some time lurking (reading posts without contributing) to understand the dynamics before jumping into discussions. LinkedIn groups such as "Artificial Intelligence, Deep Learning, Machine Learning: Networking & AI Jobs" provide a more professional setting to connect with industry experts, find job opportunities, and gain insights into the AI market trends. For real-time interaction and more community-driven support, Discord servers like the "AI & Data Science Community" offer channels for immediate feedback and help, along with more casual interactions that help build strong network ties.

The benefits of engaging with these communities are manifold. First, they provide a support structure that can help simplify aspects of AI and ChatGPT that might initially seem overwhelming. Whether it's understanding complex algorithms, getting feedback on why your code isn't working, or simply observing conversations about AI, there's always someone who may have faced a similar issue and can offer a solution. This peer support accelerates your learning process and can also boost your confidence as you navigate your AI journey. Additionally, these communities often share the latest news, research papers, and resources, keeping you updated on the newest developments and innovations, which is crucial in a field as dynamic as AI.

Contributing to discussions is not just about asking questions but also about sharing your knowledge and experiences. Even as a beginner, you might have insights or fresh perspectives that can be valuable to others. Engaging actively in these communities helps others and establishes your presence and reputation within the community. This can lead to collaborative opportunities like working on projects with other members or forming study groups and partnerships. Over time, regular contributions can also establish you as a thought leader in specific AI niches, opening doors to professional opportunities and collaborations.

Furthermore, networking in these AI and ChatGPT-focused groups can be incredibly beneficial. You might connect with potential mentors who can provide guidance and advice, or you might encounter potential employers interested in the skills and knowledge you demonstrate in your interactions. Networking can also lead to opportunities to attend or speak at conferences and seminars, further expanding your understanding and professional network. Remember, every post you read, every discussion you contribute to, and every connection you make is a step toward not just learning but becoming an integral part of the AI community.

By joining and participating in AI and ChatGPT forums and social media groups, you gain access to a wealth of knowledge and resources and contribute to a growing field that thrives on shared learning and collaboration. These communities offer a space to learn, teach, network, and grow, providing a comprehensive ecosystem supporting your personal and professional development in AI.

7.3 Attending Workshops and Webinars for Hands-On Learning

Finding the right workshops and webinars that align with your skill level and interests in AI and ChatGPT can significantly enhance your learning experience. These events, often filled with interactive sessions and live demonstrations, provide a platform to deepen your understanding and apply what you've learned in real-time scenarios. Check out platforms like Eventbrite or Meetup, which host many tech-focused events, to locate these valuable learning opportunities. You can filter your search by topics such as ChatGPT, AI, or machine learning to find events that match your interests. Additionally, following industry leaders or organizations on social media platforms can keep you informed about upcoming webinars and workshops. Many universities and tech companies regularly host such events and often offer them for free or at a minimal cost to encourage participation from a broad audience.

There are many advantages to engaging in these hands-on learning environments. Firstly, they provide a dynamic setting to apply theoretical knowledge. Imagine participating in a workshop where you learn about the intricacies of neural networks and experiment with them through guided exercises. This practical application cements your understanding and aids in retaining information much more effectively than passive learning methods. Moreover, workshops and webinars often introduce real-world problems, allowing you to employ AI solutions in practical scenarios. This boosts your problem-solving skills and prepares you for challenges you might face in professional settings. The interactive nature of these events also means you can receive immediate feedback on your work, which is invaluable as it provides insights into areas for improvement and reaffirms concepts that you've mastered.

Engaging directly with experts and speakers at these events can dramatically enrich your learning journey. These interactions allow you to gain insights from individuals at the forefront of AI technology and innovation. For instance, a casual conversation during a workshop break might provide you with a new perspective on deploying ChatGTP within your projects, or a question-and-answer session might clear up longstanding confusion about certain AI functionalities. Experts can also offer personalized advice tailored to your specific interests and challenges, which is often not possible through other learning mediums. Their experience and knowledge can guide you in focusing on skills and areas most beneficial for your career or personal growth in AI.

Attending these workshops and webinars is crucial for keeping your skills and knowledge current. AI and technologies like ChatGPT evolve at a breakneck pace, with new advancements and updates emerging regularly. By making it a habit to participate in relevant events, you remain current with the latest technologies, methodologies, and best practices. This ongoing engagement helps in personal growth and enhances your professional value, making you a sought-after asset in tech-centric roles. Furthermore, regular attendance helps build a professional network with other AI enthusiasts and experts, which can benefit collaborative opportunities and career advancement.

In summary, workshops and webinars offer a structured yet flexible approach to learning that can significantly enhance your proficiency in AI and ChatGPT. By actively seeking out events that align with your learning goals, engaging with experts, and committing to continuous education, you equip yourself with the tools needed to excel in the fast-evolving world of artificial intelligence. Whether you are a beginner looking to get your feet wet or a seasoned professional aiming to update your skills, these hands-on learning experiences are invaluable resources that propel you toward your goals.

7.4 Subscribing to Newsletters and Following AI Thought Leaders

In the fast-evolving field of artificial intelligence, staying updated with the latest trends, breakthroughs, and insights is crucial. Subscribing to well-curated newsletters and following respected thought leaders in AI can provide a steady stream of valuable information, helping you keep pace with developments, deepen your understanding, and enhance your professional capabilities. When selecting quality sources for AI newsletters, look for well-researched, timely, and diverse content. Publications like 'The Algorithm' by MIT Technology Review, 'Import AI' by Jack Clark, and 'The Rundown AI' provide insightful analyses and cover various topics, from technical advancements to ethical discussions and the latest news. These newsletters should ideally blend theoretical knowledge with practical insights, offering you a comprehensive view of the AI landscape.

Identifying influential thought leaders in the AI community involves looking for individuals who have expertise and actively contribute to the field through research, innovation, and education. Figures like Andrew Ng, founder of Coursera and a pioneer in machine learning, and Fei-Fei Li, a leading AI researcher and advocate for diversity in technology, are excellent examples. Following these leaders on platforms like Twitter or LinkedIn allows you to gain insights from their research, projects, and commentary on industry trends. Engaging with their shared content can significantly enhance your understanding and inspire your work in AI.

Keeping abreast of industry trends through these newsletters and thought leaders helps you understand the trajectory of AI technologies and their broader implications for various sectors. This knowledge is not just academically interesting—it's practically essential. In professional settings, the insights gained from these sources can inform decision-making processes and strategic planning. For example, understanding the latest advancements in natural language processing could lead you to implement AI-driven solutions like ChatGPT more effectively within your business operations, enhancing efficiency and customer satisfaction.

Moreover, embracing a diversity of perspectives in AI is vital. Artificial intelligence is technical and profoundly impacts societal norms and ethical standards. By following a diverse range of voices, including those from different cultural, gender, and academic backgrounds, you gain a more holistic view of the challenges and opportunities within AI. This diversity enriches your understanding and supports a more comprehensive approach to implementing AI solutions, considering various ethical dimensions and cultural implications that could affect the deployment and acceptance of AI technologies.

By subscribing to a selection of meticulously chosen newsletters and following esteemed AI thought leaders, you arm yourself with the knowledge and insights necessary to navigate the complex world of artificial intelligence. This ongoing educational process enhances your professional growth and equips you with the tools to contribute thoughtfully to discussions and innovations in the AI community. As AI continues to reshape our world, staying informed and engaged with leading sources and experts is invaluable to your growth and participation in this dynamic field.

7.5 Implementing Regular ChatGPT Training Sessions

Establishing a regular training schedule for ChatGPT is akin to setting up a fitness regimen for your mind dedicated to enhancing your AI skills. The key is consistency and progression. Begin by carving out specific time devoted to working with ChatGPT in your week. This could be as little as an hour every other day or perhaps a more intensive two-hour session once a week, depending on your current schedule and commitments. The importance lies not in the quantity but in the quality and regularity of these sessions. Stick to these times as you would a class or a business meeting, underscoring the importance of this commitment to yourself.

Having clear learning objectives in each session can significantly enhance your productivity and focus. Start by identifying what you wish to achieve at the end of each training session. For beginners, objectives might include understanding basic ChatGPT functionalities, such as learning how to set up the AI or initiate basic interactions. More advanced users might focus on exploring specific features, like fine-tuning the model for particular tasks or delving into more complex prompt engineering techniques. Setting these targets before each session guides your activities and provides a clear measure of success at the end of your training period.

Incorporating real-world scenarios into your ChatGPT training sessions can dramatically enhance your understanding and practical skills. For instance, if you are in marketing, you could use ChatGPT to craft compelling content or generate creative taglines for products. If you're in customer service, simulate various customer interactions to understand better how ChatGPT can handle inquiries, complaints, or feedback. These scenarios make your sessions more engaging and ensure that the skills you are developing are directly applicable to your real-life professional challenges. This practical application cements your learning and empowers you to see the potential impacts of AI in your everyday work, making the training sessions both educational and rewarding.

Tracking your progress is crucial in maintaining motivation and measuring the effectiveness of your training sessions. One effective method is to maintain a learning journal where you document your objectives, the processes, and the outcomes of each session. Reflecting on what was learned, what challenges emerged, and how they were addressed can provide valuable insights into your learning journey and highlight areas that need more focus or adjustment. Additionally, leveraging digital tools like online quizzes or AI skill assessments can provide quantitative measures of your progress. These tools often offer feedback on areas of strength and improvement, allowing for targeted learning in subsequent sessions. Regularly reviewing your progress ensures that your training remains aligned with your learning goals, adjusting your strategies as needed to optimize learning outcomes.

Through these structured training sessions, you enhance your ability to use ChatGPT effectively and deepen your overall understanding of AI technologies. This ongoing commitment to learning and improvement is essential in keeping pace with the rapid developments in AI, ensuring that you remain proficient and competitive in leveraging AI tools like ChatGPT. Whether you are advancing in your career or simply satisfying your curiosity about AI, these regular training sessions provide a solid foundation for growth and mastery in the ever-evolving landscape of artificial intelligence.

7.6 Innovating with ChatGPT: Experimenting with New Uses

In the ever-evolving landscape of artificial intelligence, the ability to think outside the box and explore uncharted territories with tools like ChatGPT can set you apart from the rest. This section is dedicated to inspiring you to think creatively about how you can employ ChatGPT in ways that perhaps haven't been discussed in previous chapters. Imagine ChatGPT not just as a tool for answering queries or automating tasks but as a canvas for creativity. Have you considered, for example, using ChatGPT to create unique learning experiences for students in remote areas or perhaps to develop interactive narratives for online gaming? The potential applications are as varied as they are exciting. This exploration begins with a mindset open to experimentation and a willingness to try new ideas, no matter how unconventional they may seem.

Documenting your experiments with ChatGPT is crucial in understanding what works and what doesn't. It's similar to keeping a lab notebook in scientific research. Every detail of your experiments, including your prompt designs, the responses from ChatGPT, and any modifications you make, should be meticulously recorded. This practice allows you to track your progress and helps pinpoint the exact factors that lead to successful outcomes or unexpected failures. For instance, if you're using ChatGPT to help compose music, documenting the prompts that led to the most harmonious compositions can provide insights into patterns or keywords that resonate well with the AI's algorithms. Over time, this detailed record becomes a valuable resource for refining your techniques and can significantly speed up your learning curve.

Sharing your findings with the broader AI community is another step that can amplify your impact and contribute to the collective knowledge base. Platforms like GitHub or even social media groups dedicated to AI innovation are excellent venues for disseminating your work. By publishing your experiments and outcomes, you invite feedback that can provide new perspectives and ideas you might not have considered. This collaborative approach enhances your projects and encourages a culture of openness and innovation in the AI community. Feedback from diverse sources can improve your methods and even spark new experiments, pushing the boundaries of what you can achieve with ChatGPT.

Iterative testing and refinement form the backbone of successful innovation with AI. This process involves continuously tweaking your experiments based on the results and feedback you gather. Each iteration should aim to improve upon the previous version, whether it's adjusting the complexity of the prompts, the data used for training, or the parameters of the AI model. For example, suppose you are experimenting with using ChatGPT for customer service. In that case, you might start with basic queries and then gradually introduce more complex scenarios based on how well the AI performs in each round of testing. This systematic approach ensures that your application of ChatGPT becomes more refined and effective with each cycle. Remember, innovation is not a one-time event but a continuous exploration, testing, and improvement journey. Each iteration brings you closer to discovering novel and impactful ways to utilize ChatGPT, broadening the horizons of what you can accomplish with this powerful tool.

7.7 Reviewing and Reflecting: Best Practices for ChatGPT Usage

Regular review sessions for ChatGPT usage are crucial to maintaining and enhancing its effectiveness in the dynamic and ever-evolving landscape of artificial intelligence. These sessions are routine health checks that help ensure your AI tool remains in top condition and aligned with your goals and needs. By periodically evaluating how ChatGPT is utilized within your operations—be it in business, education, or personal projects—you can identify strengths to build upon and areas that may require improvement. For instance, you might discover that while ChatGPT excels in handling customer service inquiries, it might not be as efficient in managing more complex technical support questions. These insights allow you to adjust your usage strategies or provide additional training to the model on specific topics. Implementing these review sessions monthly or quarterly can keep your AI initiatives well-aligned with your operational goals and responsive to the needs of your users.

Compiling and adhering to a set of best practice guidelines for ChatGPT usage is another cornerstone in optimizing your interactions with this AI tool. Expert advice, user feedback, and your experiences with the AI should shape these guidelines. For example, one best practice might involve setting clear parameters for the types of tasks ChatGPT handles based on its demonstrated strengths and limitations. Another might dictate how to effectively integrate human oversight in ChatGPT's processes to ensure the accuracy and appropriateness of its outputs. Drawing on community feedback is particularly valuable; users often provide insights into unique or unexpected ways the tool can be optimized that you might not have considered. Regularly updating these best practices as you gather more data and insights from ongoing usage and as new updates and features of ChatGPT are released ensures that your approach remains cutting-edge and relevant.

Fostering a culture of learning from past errors or inefficiencies in ChatGPT interactions also plays an essential role in enhancing future performance. This involves more than merely correcting mistakes—it's about understanding why errors occurred and how similar issues can be prevented going forward. For instance, if a review session reveals that ChatGPT frequently misinterprets the intent behind user queries, leading to incorrect or irrelevant responses, you might look into improving the training data or tweaking the model's context sensitivity. Encouraging your team to openly discuss and analyze these missteps, perhaps through regular brainstorming sessions or debriefs, can turn these learning experiences into opportunities for growth and innovation. This proactive approach improves the tool's efficiency and empowers your team by valuing their insights and encouraging a collaborative effort toward continuous improvement.

Lastly, staying ethically aligned when using ChatGPT cannot be overstated. As AI continues to integrate deeper into various aspects of life and business, ensuring its application adheres to ethical guidelines is paramount. This means regularly revisiting and possibly revising the ethical frameworks you have in place to govern ChatGPT's deployment in your operations. These ethical considerations are fundamental, whether it's about ensuring data privacy, avoiding bias in AI-generated content, or maintaining transparency about AI's role and limitations in your services. They protect you and your users and build trust and credibility in your AI applications. Integrating ethics into your regular review sessions, perhaps by including an ethics checklist or audit, ensures that these considerations remain at the forefront of your AI strategy. In doing so, you underscore your commitment to responsible AI usage that respects user rights and societal norms, reinforcing a positive and sustainable integration of AI technologies like ChatGPT into your operational ecosystem.

7.8 Anticipating Future Trends in AI and ChatGPT

Staying ahead in the dynamic field of artificial intelligence requires a proactive approach, where monitoring the latest technological advances is not just beneficial—it's essential. Keeping abreast of developments that could influence the capabilities and applications of AI, like ChatGPT, involves more than casual observation; it necessitates active engagement with various informational resources. Technology blogs, AI research publications, and industry news platforms are invaluable. These sources often provide early insights into emerging technologies, experimental AI applications, and potential updates to existing systems like ChatGPT. By regularly engaging with these resources, you can better understand where AI technology is headed and how it's evolving, ensuring that you're always prepared for the next big thing.

Predictive analysis plays a critical role in understanding future trends in AI. This involves analyzing current data and developments to forecast future directions in AI technology. For instance, by examining the increasing integration of AI in healthcare, one can predict a continued focus on developing AI systems that support diagnostic processes and provide personalized treatment recommendations. Similarly, the rise in the use of AI for enhancing customer service experiences suggests that future developments might focus on improving the emotional intelligence of AI systems like ChatGPT, enabling them to respond more sensitively to human emotions. Engaging in predictive analysis allows you to anticipate these trends and prepare accordingly, whether through acquiring new skills, adapting business strategies, or innovating new applications for AI.

Preparing for changes in the AI landscape is another crucial strategy for staying relevant and effective in your AI endeavors. This preparation involves learning new skills and adapting existing ones to align with how AI technologies evolve. For example, as AI systems become more autonomous, understanding the underlying principles of AI ethics and governance becomes as important as technical skills. Additionally, as AI tools like ChatGPT become more sophisticated and capable of handling complex tasks, developing AI system integration and management skills may become necessary. By continuously updating your skill set and staying flexible in your approach to AI, you can ensure that your capabilities remain in demand, regardless of how AI technologies evolve.

Global events and shifts in policy also significantly impact the evolution of AI. For instance, regulatory changes concerning data privacy can influence how AI systems are designed and used, particularly in regions with strict data protection laws. Similarly, global events such as pandemics or economic downturns can shift the focus of AI applications from commercial to humanitarian or crisis management roles. Being aware of these global dynamics and understanding their implications for AI can help you better anticipate and adapt to changes in the field. This might involve developing AI solutions that are compliant with new regulations or redirecting AI research and development efforts to address pressing global challenges.

By actively monitoring technological advances, engaging in predictive analysis, preparing for change, and understanding the influence of global events, you can confidently navigate the ever-changing landscape of AI. This proactive stance enhances your ability to use AI effectively and positions you as a forward-thinking participant in artificial intelligence, ready to adapt and thrive no matter what the future holds.

7.9 Becoming a ChatGPT Power User: Tips and Secrets

Elevating your skills with ChatGPT involves more than just routine use; it requires delving into advanced configurations, leveraging APIs, discovering hidden features, and engaging actively within the AI community. These elements are about enhancing your technical proficiency and enriching your overall experience and capabilities with this powerful AI tool.

Let's start with advanced configuration tips that can significantly enhance the efficiency and effectiveness of your ChatGPT interactions. One effective strategy is to customize the model's responses based on the context of the conversation. This can be achieved by adjusting the temperature setting in the API interface, which controls the randomness of the responses—a lower temperature results in more predictable and conservative responses suitable for formal or business communications. Conversely, a higher temperature setting allows for more creative and expansive responses, which is ideal for brainstorming sessions or when seeking innovative ideas. Additionally, tweaking the max tokens setting can help manage the length of each response, ensuring that the outputs are neither too terse nor overly verbose, perfectly matching the needs of your specific application.

The power of ChatGPT isn't just confined to what's built into it; by leveraging APIs, you can extend its capabilities and integrate it more deeply into your personal or professional projects. APIs allow ChatGPT to interact with other software and databases, enabling a seamless flow of information across platforms. For instance, integrating ChatGPT with a CRM system can automate and personalize customer interactions based on historical data, significantly enhancing customer engagement and satisfaction. Similarly, coupling ChatGPT with analytical tools can provide real-time insights from raw data, aiding in quicker decision-making. The key to effective API integration lies in understanding the specific endpoints that ChatGPT can interact with and ensuring secure and efficient data transfer between systems.

Exploring the lesser-known features or 'Easter eggs' within ChatGPT can also add fun and discovery to your interactions. For example, ChatGPT can compose poems or generate creative story ideas based on a few input keywords. Often hidden or undocumented, these features can be uncovered through experimentation or tips shared by the community. They provide entertainment and inspire creativity in how you use ChatGPT for more mundane tasks, such as drafting emails or creating content.

Lastly, becoming an active contributor to the AI community can significantly enhance your status as a power user. This involves sharing your custom scripts, innovative prompt designs, or unique use cases. Platforms like GitHub or AI-focused forums are excellent venues for these contributions. Sharing your work encourages feedback, leading to improvements and new ideas while helping others face similar challenges. Contributing to the community bolsters your knowledge and establishes your reputation as a thought leader in the AI space.

By mastering these advanced techniques and engaging with the broader AI community, you elevate your prowess with ChatGPT beyond typical usage, unlocking new potentials and opportunities. This proactive approach enhances your immediate interactions with ChatGPT and prepares you for future advancements in AI technologies. As we close this chapter on keeping up with ChatGPT developments, we reflect on transforming from a novice to an advanced user. The tips and secrets shared here are your tools for deepening your understanding and enhancing your skills.

7.10 Interactive Task

To summarize this chapter and solidify your understanding, create a personalized plan to stay updated with AI and ChatGPT advancements. Identify an essential resource from the chapter that resonates with your interests or professional goals. This could include subscribing to a specific newsletter, joining a particular forum or social media group, or attending a webinar or workshop. Outline how you will engage with these resources regularly, whether daily, weekly, or monthly. Additionally, set a goal to experiment with at least one new use case for ChatGPT each month, using the insights and tips provided in this book. Reflect on your progress and experiences in a dedicated journal, noting any new skills acquired or challenges faced. This ongoing commitment will ensure you remain at the forefront of AI developments, maximize the potential of ChatGPT in your personal and professional life, and provide interesting topics for AI conversations around the water cooler.

Keeping the Knowledge Alive

Now you have everything you need to master ChatGPT and unlock its full potential, it's time to pass on your newfound knowledge and show other readers where they can find the same help.

By leaving your honest opinion of this book on Amazon, you'll show other beginners where they can find the information they're looking for and pass on your passion for ChatGPT.

I appreciate your help. The excitement and utility of ChatGPT are kept alive when we pass on our knowledge – and you're helping us to do just that.

Simply click or scan the QR code below to leave your review on Amazon:

Conclusion

As we reach the end of this enriching journey together, reflecting on the path we've traversed is remarkable. From the initial steps of understanding what AI and ChatGPT are to delving into their intricate workings and exploring how they can be seamlessly integrated into our daily lives, this book has been a voyage of simplifying AI, especially ChatGPT, transforming what may once have appeared as a complex subject into accessible and actionable knowledge.

For beginners, the realm of AI can seem daunting; however, this guide was meticulously crafted with you in mind, aiming to empower you with the confidence to navigate this technological landscape. By breaking down complex concepts and providing step-by-step applications, I hope you feel equipped to utilize ChatGPT effectively, enhancing your personal and professional endeavors.

Throughout our discussions, we've strongly emphasized the importance of ethical AI use. Engaging responsibly with AI technologies like ChatGPT is crucial, ensuring their application aligns with ethical standards and contributes positively to society. This understanding is foundational and essential for fostering a future where technology enhances human capabilities without compromising moral values.

The skills you've acquired—crafting effective prompts, integrating AI into everyday tasks, and keeping abreast of ongoing advancements—are more than just technical competencies; they empower you to innovate and create. Whether optimizing your workflow, enhancing your learning, or exploring new creative avenues, these skills are your stepping stones to success in an AI-driven world.

However, the journey doesn't end here. I encourage you to continue learning and experimenting with ChatGPT. AI is ever-evolving, and staying engaged through continuous education and hands-on practice is vital to maintaining relevance and expertise. Join AI and ChatGPT communities, where you can share knowledge, gain insights, and network with peers who are equally passionate about this exciting technology.

As you apply the insights and skills from this book, challenge yourself to think outside the box. Innovate in your professional field, streamline processes, enhance communications, or even solve complex problems that you encounter. The possibilities are limitless when you leverage AI responsibly and creatively.

Looking ahead, the future of AI and technologies like ChatGPT holds incredible potential. With advancements in machine learning and natural language processing, we are on the cusp of witnessing even more transformative changes that can bring about significant societal benefits. It is a future ripe with opportunities, and by using AI responsibly, we can all contribute to a world where technology and humanity progress hand in hand.

I invite you to share your experiences, challenges, and successes as you venture further into AI. Your feedback is invaluable to me and others in the community who can learn from your journey. Engage through social media, online forums, or the dedicated book website. Your insights will help shape the ongoing dialogue about AI and its role in our lives.

Thank you for joining me on this educational adventure. Your commitment to understanding and leveraging AI is a personal achievement and a step forward for us all in navigating this dynamic digital age. Let's continue to explore, innovate, and lead in this exciting field together.

References

Author unknown. (n.d.). What is AI technology? *Dummies.com*. Retrieved from https://www.dummies.com/article/technology/information-technolog y/ai/general-ai/4-ways-define-artificial-intelligence-ai-254174/

OpenAI. (n.d.). Introducing ChatGPT. *OpenAI*. Retrieved from https://ope nai.com/index/chatgpt/

CallMiner. (n.d.). 25 examples of NLP & machine learning in everyday life. Retrieved from https://callminer.com/blog/25-examples-of-nlp-and-machin e-learning-in-everyday-life

Walsh, C. (2020, October 20). Ethical concerns mount as AI takes bigger decision-making role. *Harvard Gazette*. Retrieved from https://news.harvard.edu/gazette/story/2020/10/ethical-concerns-mou nt-as-ai-takes-bigger-decision-making-role/

GPTBot.io. (n.d.). Mastering ChatGPT: How to craft effective prompts (full guide). Retrieved from https://gptbot.io/master-chatgpt-prompting-techniq ues-guide/

Marr, B. (2023, May 30). 10 amazing real-world examples of how companies are using ChatGPT in 2023. *Forbes*. Retrieved from https://www.forbes.com/sites/bernardmarr/2023/05/30/10-amazing-r eal-world-examples-of-how-companies-are-using-chatgpt-in-2023/

McKinsey & Company. (n.d.). Tackling bias in artificial intelligence (and in humans). Retrieved from https://www.mckinsey.com/featured-insights/artificial-intelligence/tackling-bias-in-artificial-intelligence-and-in-humans

Aphelion Group. (n.d.). Unleashing innovation: The power of AI in creative problem solving. *Medium*. Retrieved from https://medium.com/@AphelionGroup/unleashing-innovation-the-power-of-ai-in-creative-problem-solving-9a2e27af27de

TechTarget. (n.d.). 10 realistic business use cases for ChatGPT. Retrieved from https://www.techtarget.com/searchenterpriseai/tip/Realistic-business-use-cases-for-ChatGPT

Sitecore. (n.d.). How to use AI in email marketing: A practical guide. Retrieved from https://www.sitecore.com/knowledge-center/digital-marketing-resources/how-to-use-ai-in-email-marketing-a-practical-guide

SEMrush. (n.d.). AI in content creation: Best practices & top tools for 2024. Retrieved from https://www.semrush.com/goodcontent/content-marketing-blog/ai-content-marketing/#:~=AI%20content%20creation%20is%20the,useful%20audience%20insights%2C%20and%20more

Schaefer, M. (2023, February 15). How to integrate ChatGPT with your CRM software. *Webbiquity*. Retrieved from https://webbiquity.com/ai-in-marketing/how-to-integrate-chatgpt-with-your-crm-software/

Abdolrauf, A. (2023, March 22). 20 powerful ChatGPT productivity tools, apps, & extensions. Retrieved from https://abdolrauf.com/chatgpt-productivity-tools/

Simplilearn. (n.d.). Advantages and disadvantages of artificial intelligence [AI]. Retrieved from https://www.simplilearn.com/advantages-and-disadvantages-of-artificial-intelligence-article#:~

=While%20artificial%20intelligence%20has%20many,the%20advancement%20of%20autonomous%20vehicles

CNET. (2024, January 10). How AI could shake up your future fitness routine. Retrieved from https://www.cnet.com/health/fitness/ai-in-fitness-could-your-future-workout-buddy-be-a-robot/

Northern Illinois University. (n.d.). ChatGPT and education. Retrieved from https://www.niu.edu/citl/resources/guides/chatgpt-and-education.shtml

Wired. (2023, April 1). ChatGPT has a big privacy problem. Retrieved from https://www.wired.com/story/italy-ban-chatgpt-privacy-gdpr/

World Economic Forum. (2024, June 1). How AI can also be used to combat online disinformation. Retrieved from https://www.weforum.org/agenda/2024/06/ai-combat-online-misinformation-disinformation/

UNESCO. (n.d.). Ethics of artificial intelligence. Retrieved from https://www.unesco.org/en/artificial-intelligence/recommendation-ethics

OpenAI. (2023). ChatGPT — Release notes. Retrieved from https://help.openai.com/en/articles/6825453-chatgpt-release-notes

CX Today. (2023, June 12). OpenAI allows businesses to customize ChatGPT for specific use cases. Retrieved from https://www.cxtoday.com/contact-centre/openai-allows-businesses-to-customize-chatgpt-for-specific-use-cases/

Akkio. (2023, August 15). ChatGPT advanced data analysis: Guide & use cases. Retrieved from https://www.akkio.com/post/chatgpt-advanced-data-analysis

MyGreatLearning. (2024). Free ChatGPT course with certificate. Retrieved from https://www.mygreatlearning.com/academy/learn-for-free/courses/chatgpt-for-beginners

McKinsey & Company. (2023). The state of AI in 2023: Generative AI's breakout year. Retrieved from https://www.mckinsey.com/capabilities/quantumblack/our-insights/the-state-of-ai-in-2023-generative-ais-breakout-year

University of Texas at San Antonio. (2024). Is an artificial intelligence certification valuable for my career? Retrieved from https://www.utsa.edu/pace/news/artificial-intelligence-certification-valuable-for-my-career.html

The Hive Index. (2024). 17 best artificial intelligence communities to join in 2024. Retrieved from https://thehiveindex.com/topics/artificial-intelligence/

Forbes Advisor. (2024). How businesses are using artificial intelligence in 2024. Retrieved from https://www.forbes.com/advisor/business/software/ai-in-business/